AMBITIOUS POLITICIANS

AMBITIOUS POLITICIANS

The Implications of Career Ambition in
Representative Democracy

Patrik Öhberg

University Press of Kansas

Published by the University Press of Kansas (Lawrence, Kansas 66045), which was organized by the Kansas Board of Regents and is operated and funded by Emporia State University, Fort Hays State University, Kansas State University, Pittsburg State University, the University of Kansas, and Wichita State University

Translation completed by Proper English AB.

Library of Congress Cataloging-in-Publication Data

Names: Öhberg, Patrik.
Title: Ambitious politicians : the implications of career ambition in representative democracy / Patrik Öhberg.
Description: Lawrence : University Press of Kansas, 2017. | Includes bibliographical references and index.
Identifiers: LCCN 2016055778
ISBN 9780700624225 (hardback)
ISBN 9780700624232 (paperback)
ISBN 9780700624249 (ebook)
Subjects: LCSH: European Parliament. | Legislators—Europe—Attitudes. | United States. Congress. | Legislators—United States—Attitudes. | Ambition. | Representative government and representation—Europe. | Representative government and representation—United States. | Comparative government. | BISAC: POLITICAL SCIENCE / Political Process / Leadership. | POLITICAL SCIENCE / Political Process / Political Parties.
Classification: LCC JN36 .O43 2017 | DDC 328.3/3—dc23
LC record available at https://lccn.loc.gov/2016055778.
British Library Cataloguing-in-Publication Data is available.

Printed in the United States of America

10 9 8 7 6 5 4 3 2 1

The paper used in this publication is recycled and contains 30 percent postconsumer waste. It is acid free and meets the minimum requirements of the American National Standard for Permanence of Paper for Printed Library Materials Z39.48-1992.

CONTENTS

TABLES

PREFACE AND ACKNOWLEDGMENTS

A former Swedish party leader once asked me what I study. I told him that I am interested in politicians with career ambitions. "Are there really such politicians?" he replied. The question was rather telling. In Swedish political memoirs and even in Swedish political science the notion of ambitious politicians has long been frowned upon. As I have come to realize, this skepticism is not just a Swedish phenomenon but an overall European one. Ambitious politicians are somehow seen both as a problem and as something that does not even exist.

In this book, I take inspiration from the prevalent American discussion about ambition in politics, and I claim that there is a similar category of politicians who strive to become leaders of the party-centred European democracies. What is more, those politicians reach high positions and are different from those who do not: politicians with career ambitions have a distinct idea of representation. They perceive their own opinion to be of greater importance than other politicians do, and they are more active in their party's group meetings. Politicians with career ambitions are also more prone to develop a strategy that aims at being responsive to the wishes of the party elite. I also show that politicians with career ambitions are more common in some European parliaments than in others. In more equalitarian societies there are fewer politicians with career ambitions. Countries like Greece and Italy have considerably more politicians with career ambitions in their parliaments than countries like Germany and Sweden. Therefore, it would be a mistake not to consider career ambitions in analyses of party-centred democratic systems. My hope is that this book will contribute to a greater interest in and understanding of individuals who aim at—and obtain—top positions in representative democracies.

With that said, I'd like to take this opportunity to be more personal. For a period of time, I have had two odd goals in my life (among other goals, I should add). One was to bench press at least 150 kilograms (about 330 pounds), and the other was to publish the book you hold in your hands. I have now accomplished both of them. For the progression in the gym, I have to give most of the credit to myself. (Yet, I do want to thank all the guys in the gym who over the years have lifted bars off my chest when my optimism was stronger than my muscles.)

For the book, in contrast, many people deserve to be acknowledged and thanked for making the project possible. Among them, Paul Sniderman deserves special note. Paul, I am so grateful for all your efforts and for believing that this project had potential. I also want to thank my skilled and dedicated colleagues at the vibrant Department of Political Science at the University of Gothenburg. I always find it fun to go to work. A special mention goes to Peter Esaiasson and Lena Wängnerud, who once upon a time were my supervisors and who have supported me so much during the research that led to this book. A sincere thank you also goes to all the Swedish Members of Parliament (MPs) who after each election since 1985 have answered the Parliament Survey conducted at the Swedish National Election Study Program at the University of Gothenburg. Without their efforts, our research on political elites would not be possible.

An indispensable insight into the MPs' everyday life was given to me when I received a Parliamentary scholarship that made it possible for me to work in the Riksdag for a year. I am very happy for that opportunity. I am also very grateful to Riksbankens Jubileumsfond, which funded the translation of my manuscript, and to Sören Holmberg, who vouched for me during that process and who has supported me in important ways throughout this project.

Finally, it is appropriate to thank my "wingman"—Elin Naurin. It is such a privilege to have you as a colleague, coauthor, and wife. I truly believe that our best days are ahead of us, and that is to say a lot, since we have had so many good ones already. To Miranda and William: you are my wonderful darlings. I am looking forward to many more exciting endeavors and discussions about what is going on in the world—in yours and in mine.

1. Are There Ambitious Politicians among Us?

This book is about personal motivators in the lives of politicians, especially those aiming for the highest levels of the political hierarchy—ambitious politicians. At the center of interest is the potential conflict between politicians' personal ambition and their parties' collective goals. The question is, how do politicians handle their own personal ambitions in a collective context? In the United States there is a prevalence of literature on personal driving forces; in Europe there is very little. The difference is striking: whereas personal ambition is a constant in US studies of the senators and representatives of Congress, studies of European ministers of parliament (MPs) instead focus on collective party goals and institutional constraints.

Though it makes sense to put more focus on candidates' ambitions in the US context than in the European, this is no argument for not studying individual politicians' career ambition *at all* in the European party-centered contexts. Instead, the findings from within the United States clearly indicate that politicians with career ambitions make a difference. American politicians with career ambitions are strategic about when and where they campaign for office (Jacobson 1989). Moreover, they work hard to cultivate a personal relationship with their voters and to understand voters' preferences (Maestas 2003). Politicians with career ambitions also introduce more bills, are more active on the floor, and believe in legislative specialization (Herrick and Moore 1993). If there are ambitious politicians also in the national European parliaments, we should study who they are and what they do in the legislatures.

The main claim I make in this book is that individuals' drive to achieve successful careers in politics affects how representative democracy works also in party-centered systems. In a nutshell, politicians' personal driving forces deserve to be brought to the foreground of political analyses outside the American context.

This book is the first to provide a thorough study of elite politicians who aspire to the top echelons of the parliamentary system. As surprising as it may seem, there has been no previous systematic study to determine who these politicians are and how they behave in parliament. The study makes use of a unique data set that enables comparisons among eleven European parliaments. It delves especially deep into a country where parties are particularly strong and coherent: Sweden. Sweden

1

provides a case where politicians need to balance potential personal driving forces toward the collective goals formulated by their party. If personal career ambitions matter in the Swedish context, they are likely to matter also in other settings where the party places constraints on politicians—so the argument goes. Sweden offers an excellent opportunity to work with data from an exceptionally long and ambitious tradition of studying political elites (which I'll describe later in this chapter).

Chapter 1 takes the reader through the argument that reluctance toward career politicians is deeply embedded in human nature. We will see that evolutionist studies claim that individuals' ambition could threaten the group's survival. Similar arguments are found in early religious thinking as well as in early political philosophy.

Thereafter follows a description of the role of personal ambitions in Sweden along with some background on the Swedish political system. The methodological approach of the book is thereafter described, and I outline the data sources used. The specific research questions that the data enables me to pose end this first chapter.

In Chapter 2 I discuss political science theories that explain personal driving forces in politics. The American approach to personal driving forces in politics is central—in particular, Joseph Schlesinger's framework for analyses of political ambition. The chapter ends with a description of how I define and operationalize *ambition* in this book.

Chapter 3 investigates the extent to which there are MPs who aspire to high positions in party-centered parliaments. Chapter 4 asks what these highly ambitious MPs have in common and whether they come from different backgrounds compared to other politicians. Chapter 5 investigates to what extent ambitious politicians' attitudes and behavior differ from that of other politicians. And Chapter 6 zooms in on the actions of the ambitious politicians, asking whether they indeed are more successful than politicians who lack ambition. Chapter 7 discusses whether the lessons learned from the Swedish case are generalizable to other European party-centered systems. Chapter 8 summarizes and concludes the book.

COLLECTIVE GOALS VERSUS PERSONAL AMBITIONS

Political ambition has an accepted place in American political science.[1] Joseph Schlesinger, an early identifier of the effects of ambition on representative democracy, goes so far as to argue that the drive to hold office is a fundamental building block of effective democracy. "Representative government depends above all upon a supply of individuals with strong office drives. It must provide the refinements of power and status that attract as well as direct men's and women's aspirations. No more irresponsible government is imaginable than one of high-minded individuals unconcerned for their political futures" (Schlesinger 1994:35).

While it may seem both cynical and oversimplified to reduce political engagement to raw ambition, the notion of the power struggle as an expected element recurs in the theoretical discussion of good representation (Aldrich 1995; Downs 1957; Riker 1962; Schumpeter 1942). If politicians are indifferent about whether or not they stay in office, voters lose an important channel of voice (Przeworski, Stokes, and Manin 1999). This perspective has played only a minor role in Europe (Borchert and Stolz 2011). European political scientists frequently turn to major structural explanations as a route to understanding political phenomena, and it would indeed be foolish to ignore such aspects. It is equally foolish to abstain from studying whether and how the personal drives of politicians influence events surrounding the exercise of political power.

The struggle among political agents can be organized in various ways. Electoral systems that emphasize individual politicians rely on the existence of individuals with sufficiently strong office drives to orchestrate their own election campaigns and make themselves known to voters (Cox 1987; Cox and McCubbins 1993; Kiewiet and McCubbins 1991; Strøm 1990). In a party-centric system, it is instead the parties that collectively step forward and organize the fight for political power in both the electoral and parliamentary arenas (Duverger 1954; Katz and Mair 1994; Panebianco 1988; Sjöblom 1968). In such a system, the primary endeavor of political representatives might not be to achieve a career in politics, but they nonetheless work hard to help the party gain power and seats in parliament. Hypothetically, this might mean that even if striving to achieve prominent political positions is an important aspect of representative democracy, the task may be divided between the representative and the party in various configurations. In some systems, that the individuals who represent a party and fight for its victory also want personal influence is thus taken more as a matter of course, while in other systems that notion is more alien.

The American studies provide useful insights into the candidate-centered US system, but there is still much to be explained regarding the determinants of politicians with career ambitions in party-centered systems. In party-centered systems, politicians not only have to develop their relations with voters but also are highly dependent on the relationships within the party. As David Mayhew explained in *Congress: The Electoral Connection* (1974), there are important preconditions that distinguish an MP from a member of Congress. Mayhew pointed to the fact that MPs have a strong incentive to fall in line under the pressure of party cohesion because their careers depend on the prime minister's approval by the citizenry. In contrast, member of Congress have to build their own coalitions to win elections and cannot rely on their parties to do much for them. Mayhew concluded that in a party system, "The arrangement of incentives and resources elevates parties over politicians" (1974:22).

Even so, we must keep in mind that American politicians are members of parties as well. Lindstädt and Vander Wielen (2014) found that members of Congress and the party leadership have a cyclic relationship. In the beginning of an electoral term, senators and representatives are "forced" to take instructions from the leadership, but during election years they have more leverage to make their own decisions. Cox and McCubbins (2007) also found that there are constant negotiations between members of Congress and the leadership within the party. Many subtleties may be at play in the American system regarding the interactions between members of Congress and their parties and the evolution of political careers.

As we look closely at party-centered systems, we will see that the proportion of ambitious MPs varies among parliaments. Ambitious politicians are, quite simply, a universal phenomenon that we would be wise to study in order to understand what kinds of individuals gain powerful positions in representative democracies. Disregarding the differences between political systems, the subjects of ambition and which politicians citizens want to be their leaders are complicated.

In the following pages I will show that there is something deeply human about feeling ambivalent toward ambitious politicians, which also affects the structure of this book.

EVOLUTION AND AMBITION

There is growing interest in political science as it relates to genetics and basic human motivations. Research in this area is preoccupied with subjects like people's tendency to vote and the relationship between genes and political orientations (see, for example, Alford, Funk, and Hibbing 2005; Fowler and Schreiber 2008; Hatemi et al. 2007). When it comes to humans' inherited perspectives on leadership, there is intriguing research that is relevant to studies of political career ambition: much of it suggests that humans mistrust pretenders to leadership positions and have an innate drive to preserve equality between individuals. Experimental studies also show that people are disturbed by large differences in income and are willing to act to do something about it. "Emotional reactions towards high earners—even when the source of income is known to be purely random—cause individuals to engage in costly acts that promote equitable resource distributions" (Dawes et al. 2007:796).

Likewise, ethnographers have found distinct egalitarian elements and a strong dislike of interpersonal hierarchies in modern hunter-gatherer societies (Boehm

2008). When researchers have processed data from hunter-gatherer societies in various parts of the world, they have found few examples of individuals who try to grab power or position, or of leaders who try to "boss" others around (ibid., 331). According to this research, individuals who make a bid for dominance risk being punished and shunned. "When an individual departs too far from the egalitarian ethos, the entire group either turns against him and cuts him down to size, or else it simply does away with him by means of ejection from the group or through capital punishment" (ibid., 328).

One should perhaps remember that these are situations in which everyone is basically equal and leadership is voluntary on the part of the led. What makes these societies interesting in this context is that humans have been living as hunter-gatherers for 50,000 years—almost 2,000 generations. It has been estimated that it takes at least 1,000 generations to introduce a new trait (ibid., 325). This might also be one explanation of why neuroscientists studying the brains of contemporary humans find that inequality-averse social preferences are innate (Tricomi et al. 2010). Thus, it is possible that the traits that are important under these circumstances are still found in us today. Studies that underscore the human genetic propensity toward egalitarian values are relatively comprehensive (Fehr, Fischbacher, and Gächter 2002). To put it another way, there are biological reasons ambitious people should watch their tongues.

An overview of research on leadership from an evolutionary perspective points out that there is a recurring theme when it comes to the type of leadership we human beings dislike. The conclusion is that leadership that relies on dominance is bound to be problematic. It seems that "people who have the desire to lead must rely on tactics other than sheer dominance to attract followers" (Van Vugt 2006:359). In other studies where people were asked to rank various attributes in politicians, the character trait people liked the least was that of being power-hungry (Kinder et al. 1980:319). Experiments also show that people are quite adept at "exposing" ambitious people and that this process is virtually innate (Smith et al. 2007:59). There is also a gender aspect; researchers timed how long it took for subjects to connect the craving for power to gender. The subjects needed only a second or two to associate high ambition with male behavior, while there was not the same intuitive association between ambition and female behavior (ibid., 64). Overall, women were perceived as less self-interested and less ambitious than men (ibid., 67).[2]

In light of this research, it seems that leaders should not overtly express a "craving for power." It is, however, obvious that the relationship between leadership and self-interest is complex. Leadership per se may draw out a person's more selfish tendencies. Abraham Lincoln is supposed to have once said, "Nearly all men can stand adversity, but if you want to test a man's character, give him power." The problem with Lincoln's observation is that one must first give a person power in order to judge whether he or she is fit. To Lincoln's credit, there is now research indicating that there is some truth to what he said.

In social psychology, people are categorized as "proselfs" and "prosocials" (Messick and McClintock 1968). The division comes from how individuals allocate resources based on what they consider most important—themselves, others, or both. People in the proself category are primarily interested in making sure resource allocation benefits themselves, whereas the prosocials value equality and thus allocate resources differently (Stouten, De Cremer, and Van Dijk 2005). According to these studies, the differences between proselfs and prosocials do not manifest until they are allocated a leadership role; otherwise, no systematic differences can be shown. It is thus the leadership itself that induces self-benefiting behavior in some people, and it is in these situations that proselfs set themselves apart. "Indeed, the current findings now suggest that the reported increase in self-benefiting allocations should primarily be ascribed to proself leaders" (Van Dijk and De Cremer 2006:1358). *Who* becomes a leader is therefore very important. Still, there is something of a paradox here: why have we humans created hierarchical societies and invested certain offices with great power, when we mistrust people who are willing to assume these offices?[3] One answer might be that ambition is one thing, and career ambition is something else entirely. Career ambition need not be problematic, as long as the circumstances surrounding a person intent on making it to the top are the right ones.[4]

AMBITION AND LEGITIMACY

How to choose leaders has been a topic of discussion going back to ancient Greece. Plato, for example, stated that a politician with personal ambitions is the least suitable individual to govern a city (Plato 1987). Later, important thinkers such as St. Thomas Aquinas and St. Augustine viewed ambition as a vice, a powerful force that might make individuals search for glory and in so doing forsake God (Houser 2002; Weststeijn 2010). Thomas More, influenced by ancient philosophers, imagined a model society—Utopia—in which the institutions created by the Utopians "extirpated the roots of ambition and factionalism along with all other vices" (as quoted in White 1982:347).

Other philosophers have been less skeptical toward individuals with ambitions. According to Aristotle, politics is not an exact science, which is why goodness of character is an absolute necessity. He believed there are a number of critical factors to consider when evaluating candidates for leadership positions. When someone declares interest in a representative position, take note of *when* they say they want to be a leader, when they *announce* their candidacy, *why* they say they want to be a leader, what they intend to *achieve* by their leadership, and *how* they intend to fulfill their intentions (Aristotle 2009). Aristotle's criteria caution against automatically rejecting those who seek leadership; we should instead ask *why* the person wants to be a leader.[5] His ideas continue to be relevant with regard to the attitudes of modern individuals toward politicians and their personal motivators. Thus, the ambition to lead need not be inherently problematic. People, at least in experimental studies, make a distinction between individuals whose ambition is based on their competence, including the ability to promote the collective good, and those whose ambition is based on individualistic craving for power (Larimer, Hannagan, and Smith 2007). How citizens perceive the ambition of their leaders has consequences for how they judge the ability of representatives to make wise decisions. Being able to display altruism—or at least to give the impression of being non-self-interested—may thus be advantageous to those who want to be leaders (Hardy and Van Vugt 2006). Charitable giving, for example, has been shown to strengthen the reputations of politicians (Milinski, Semmann, and Krambeck 2002). Self-sacrificing leaders also motivate others to behave in a similar way (De Cremer and Van Knippenberg 2004).[6] The important thing is to avoid the appearance of self-interest.

Political representatives who appear selfish also risk undermining the legitimacy of the political system. This conclusion was found in a study in which participants were asked to react to various types of decisions based upon information about who the decision makers were and why they decided as they did. The study showed that participants found it more difficult to accept decisions made by ambitious decision makers, regardless of the outcome. The researchers recommend that in order to strengthen the legitimacy of the political system, measures should be taken to ensure that citizens do not believe their representatives are driven solely by a desire to lead. "Those who wish to improve citizens' perceptions of governmental decisions and of decision makers, as well as increase the willingness of citizens to accept those decisions, should take steps to make it so that people believe elected officials are not in office because of a desire for authority but rather because they have earned or otherwise acquired authority without making any conscious effort to do so" (Smith et al. 2007:296).

The authors of the study actually go so far as to advocate a political system in which politicians refuse to acknowledge any career ambitions they may have, which obviously would be very different from the current situation in the United States, where candidates do not shy away from telling potential voters about their ambitions to lead. A note of interest in connection to this is that in the early US presidential elections it was considered poor taste for candidates themselves to campaign (Troy 1996). For example, William Henry Harrison refused to participate in any campaign activities before his election as president in 1840 (ibid). Earlier, the Founding Fathers stressed the importance of individual ambition while also championing the idea of egalitarianism (Reichley 2000). As they debated the nascent country's constitution, they found inspiration in the work of English republicans, including James Harrington (Sullivan 2006). In the preceding century, Harrington presented his ideas of the importance of curbing political ambition by balancing powers.

To summarize the observations: career ambition is a loaded subject. People seem to have an innate aversion to those whom they associate with ambition for power. This aversion may also contribute to undermining the legitimacy of the entire political system. In addition, ambition often is at play during legitimate power struggles both within and between political parties, further complicating the emotional charge surrounding career ambition. Personal career ambition should therefore be handled with care when studied in empirical studies.

Next, we move our attention to the Swedish context, which is well suited to the discussion of the pressure of collective norms on personal ambition.

THE "UNAMBITIOUS" SWEDISH POLITICIAN

Researchers interested in politicians with few personal driving forces and high collective party aims tend to look at Sweden. The Swedish government's *Democracy Report* doubted the very existence of politicians with career ambition, because such ambitions do not align with "the extremely party-centric political culture that still prevails in Swedish politics, where 'careerists' ... [are] ... strange birds" (Gidlund and Möller 1999:140). Sweden has strong and influential political parties that function in a parliamentary system with a low degree of separation of powers. Elections in Sweden are proportional and are held every four years using multi-member districts.[7] Turnout is relatively high, and parties organize themselves fairly consistently on a left-right scale that is known to voters (Pierre 2016). The traditional party families are Agrarians, Conservatives, Christian Democrats, Greens, Liberals, and Socialists/Social Democrats. (For an overview of Swedish politics, see Pierre 2016).

In the parliament there is an institutional arrangement that may be disadvantageous to those with personal career ambitions. In this arrangement, usually referred to as the *seniority principle,* the MPs who have sat the longest in the parliament are first in line when various posts are to be filled (Hagevi 2010). The seniority principle may be interpreted as a way of constraining MPs' career ambitions, lessening the need to compete for various positions and offices. With its strong party cohesion, emphasis on the seniority principle, and a political culture that repudiates political ambition, Sweden's parliament is a good basis for exploring the idea of personal career ambition as a motivator in political life.

Depictions of politicians unsullied by ambition are common in the Swedish memoir literature. Many high-ranking Swedish politicians have written memoirs that attest to the fact that they did not personally struggle to gain elected positions. Alf Svensson, former chair of the Christian Democrats, is one example. Svensson refuted the notion that he had any personal ambition to become the party leader. "People around the country had been urging and pushing me to do it. If the party wanted to entrust me with the position, I should put myself at the party's service. I took on this unglamorous task out of loyalty, not careerism" (Svensson 2001:6).

Another example is the former chair of the Conservative Party, Gösta Bohman, who quoted a colleague who was putting pressure on him when he described how he was induced to run as the opposition candidate for the position of party leader: "You have to do it. If you decline, there will be serious consequences for the party. To put it bluntly, you owe it to the party" (Bohman 1983:18).

In a similar vein, former minister of finance Anne Wibble wrote in her book, *Two Cigs and a Cup of Coffee*, that it was not herself but party strategists who put her forward as minister of finance in 1991 (Wibble 1994:12). Gunnar Sträng, who served as the Swedish minister of finance for twenty-one years, had to be asked three times by Prime Minister Per Albin Hansson before he would agree to join the Social Democratic cabinet in 1945 (Johansson 1992:400ff). As one could read in the minutes of the meeting of the board of directors of the Farm Workers Union, "The chairman of the union (Sträng), after having declined the offer to become minister of agriculture for the government, had upon being urged to do so accepted a post as a consultative member of the cabinet" (ibid., 402).

In his interviews with journalist Erik Fichtelius, former prime minister Göran Persson described how he had been in denial, refusing to understand that he would be the new party leader and prime minister. His feelings at the time were, "This is not going to work, I am going to be forced into this, you can see that, you can certainly understand that. That crystal clear insight that this is going to be an utter failure" (Fichtelius 2007:27). Other politicians are quick to point out their own shortcomings. Birger Schlaug, former Green Party spokesperson, described how he ended up in that position: "Following the 1985 election, I became the spokesperson because no one else was willing to do it. It was totally bizarre because I was not only agoraphobic, I stuttered. But I had qualifications like the beard, the jeans, and the anorak" (Schlaug 2002).

These examples do not, of course, mean that ambitious politicians are absent from the Swedish political system, but they do indicate the relative caution Swedish politicians use in forging their career paths. One book on party cultures surmised that MPs should not overtly declare their ambitions: "People believe that if a Social Democrat were to say 'I would love to take on that job,' they would also instantly have declared themselves 'politically dead.' If you propose yourself for an office, you will not only lose that one, but also the next" (Barrling Hermansson 2004:173). As a representative of the Conservative Party noted in that same book, "Keeping a low profile works to your advantage and people who openly display ambition do not become popular in the group" (ibid., 103).

A similar argument is made in the published diaries of former Conservative Party chair Ulf Adelsohn, which cover the period during which he headed the party. He described the ins and outs surrounding who would succeed him in the position, which turned out to be Carl Bildt. Adelsohn wrote that Bildt had shown no personal interest in the job of party leader, but Anders Wijkman had. According to Adelsohn, Wijkman put himself forward and positioned himself, but in so doing demonstrated that he was not fit for the position. "All my experience [tells me] that those who are not hungry for a job are the best ones to do it. The hungry should in general not be called upon" (Adelsohn 1987:378). When Håkan Juholt took over as Social Democratic Party leader in 2011, he took Adelsohn's tack. At the press conference when Juholt was introduced as the nominating committee's choice, he said regarding his own career ambitions, "Anyone who has been dreaming of taking on this role would be most unsuitable" (*Svenska Dagbladet,* 11 March 2011).

The importance of maintaining a clear distinction between personal ambitions as an individual candidate and how these ambitions are expressed also emerges in one of the open-ended answers received in the 1998 Parliamentary Study.[8] One survey respondent gave the following reason for choosing not to run a personal election campaign: "I would like to be more straightforward and more personal than the unwritten 'tall poppy' laws allow. [But] the old boy network would crush me if I got more attention than them" (Parliamentary Study 1998).[9]

It is said that even former prime minister Olof Palme, despite his status as the obvious heir apparent to Tage Erlander, regretted not having strongly enough repudiated the idea of becoming the head of the Social Democratic Party. "I made the mistake of saying that I would not avoid the party's mandate to become the chair. Sträng, Rune Johansson and the others were smarter. They simply said they were not interested. That made me look like a climber" (Strand 1980:18).

The Swedish memoir literature shows that Sweden is an intriguing subject for someone who seeks to answer the question of whether personal ambition in politics is a motivator that also has impact in profoundly collectivist settings. All in all, it makes sense to see Sweden not only as an example of a party-centered system but as one where the party is very important and where politicians themselves are reluctant to talk about career ambitions. If there are ambitious MPs in the Swedish parliament, it is reasonable to presume they exist in other European parliaments as well. The Swedish case also lends perspective to American research, where ambition is described as the engine of representative democracy. A study of career ambition among politicians in Sweden permits analysis based on a system not previously studied while feeding the theoretical and normative discussion of what role personal ambition actually plays in representative democracy—and also how that ambition should be encouraged and constrained.

SOURCE MATERIAL

To enable this study of career ambition among Swedish members of parliament, I have used material from the Parliamentary Studies collected by the Department of Political Science at the University of Gothenburg. From an international perspective, the Parliamentary Studies are an extraordinary source.[10] Surveys have gone out after each parliamentary election since 1985 (with the exception of 1991). They are based on a long-standing tradition of the election study program in Sweden. Swedish MPs are unusually acquiescent about responding to these surveys. The Parliamentary Studies carried out in Gothenburg manage to achieve a response rate among MPs of above 90 percent, which makes Sweden a virtually unique case to study.

Even though the Parliamentary Studies have asked MPs hundreds of questions over the years, only once has a question dealt with MPs' career ambitions (which presumably reflects the general view on the significance of personal ambition among MPs). This occurred in 1996, an aptly chosen occasion. The 1996 Parliamentary Study was part of a European project that covered eleven European countries: Belgium, France, Germany, Greece, Ireland, Italy, Luxembourg, Netherlands, Portugal, Spain, and Sweden. This data offers an opportunity not only to study ambition among Swedish MPs but also to compare the state of affairs in the Swedish parliament to the situation elsewhere in Europe. The MPs who participated in the 1996 survey answered questions that had to do with their aspirations in ten years, which provided an opportunity to meticulously track what had happened in these MPs' careers a decade later.

I augmented the survey material from 1996 with the 1994 Parliamentary Study in which "my" respondents participated. Thanks to generous colleagues, I also had access to the material collected in the *Exit Riksdagen* study undertaken by Shirin Ahlbäck Öberg, Jörgen Hermansson, and Lena Wängnerud. *Exit Riksdagen* studied the reasons such a large proportion of the MPs in office during the 1994–1998 term did not remain in parliament for another term.

RESEARCH QUESTIONS AND ORGANIZATION
OF THE BOOK

My research focused on two general questions, one empirical and the second methodological. The first was whether ambition is an effective motivator in the Swedish parliament, the Riksdag. The second concerned the difficulties of studying personal ambition in collective settings: am I really studying what I am interested in—ambitious politicians?

First Level of Analysis

There are four main empirical questions that will be addressed at the first level of my research:

Who are the MPs that state they have career ambitions? This question will focus mainly on the relationship between the MPs' socioeconomic resources and ambition, a subject that will be dealt with in Chapter 4.

How do MPs with career ambitions act in the parliament? In Chapter 5 the aim is to see how MPs orient in the parliament and to what extent they cultivate a personal profile.

Do ambitions further MPs' careers? Because Swedish MPs declare that politicians with career ambitions do not have a place in politics, this claim is scrutinized in Chapter 6, where the parliamentarians' careers are followed for a period of ten years.

Does the share of MPs with career ambitions vary between European parliaments? In Chapter 7 Swedish MPs will be compared to other European parliamentarians. This chapter will also serve as a test of the assumption that Sweden is an interesting case because ambitious politicians are a less prevalent phenomenon. For the book to make valid claims to generalizability there should be fewer ambitious MPs in the Swedish parliament than there are in other European parliaments.

Second Level of Analysis

The desire to pursue a career in politics is something found "in the heads of MPs." As having career ambition is a controversial issue, I cannot presume that politicians will answer truthfully to questions concerning future positions. Therefore, my research strategy at the second level is focused on methodology, where the query is: *Do the survey questions identify genuinely career-minded politicians?*

A number of tests are performed to confirm the validity of the survey material with respect to the MPs' ambitions. More specifically, I establish a criterion that must be met to characterize a politician as ambitious. In short, an ambitious politician must be someone who is: (1) committed over the long term, (2) goal-oriented, (3) working toward something difficult to attain, and (4) acting to achieve the object of ambition. These criteria are presented in more detail in Chapter 2.

Each of the empirical chapters engages in the question of to what extent the survey material and the MPs' responses correspond to the demands imposed by criteria. In Chapter 3 I test the survey data to make sure that they meet the criteria I use when defining ambitious politicians. The chapter can therefore conclude that a number of Swedish politicians report having career ambition according to the definitions that I will outline in Chapter 2. Chapter 4 examines whether these MPs are in earnest about their ambitions for high-ranking positions. I do this by studying whether there are circumstances that systematically indicate that MPs who want to attain high positions differ from their colleagues in terms of prior experience. The validity test then proceeds and is concluded in Chapter 5. This is done on the basis of the criterion that to be considered ambitious, MPs must be acting to achieve their goals.

Before this work commences, I will present in the next chapter a brief summary of the conclusions of prior research on political ambition. Thereafter, I present the criteria for characterizing individual politicians as ambitious.

2. Political Ambition Theory

What actually drives our political leaders? In this chapter I will provide a brief recapitulation of what political scientists over the years have had to say about the motivations of politicians. In fact, it is almost only American scholars who have studied the subject. In the final section of the chapter I use this literature to outline my definition of what should characterize a politician with career ambitions.

POLITICAL MOTIVATIONS FROM AN AMERICAN PERSPECTIVE

What motivates politicians has been the object of both normative and empirical studies (see, e.g., Barber 1985; Faulkner 2007; Payne et al. 1984). Attention to political motivation was actualized in the early 1900s and centered on leadership analysis before, during, and after the two world wars. One reason for the focus on the individual agent was the experiences of the era with charismatic leaders. It was a relatively simple matter to drive home the thesis that individual motivations play an important role. For this reason, political leaders and their psychological dispositions were an obvious subject for social scientists.

One of the pioneers was Harold Lasswell. He did not hold politicians' motives in high esteem, as is evident in the title of his 1930 book, *Psychopathology and Politics*. According to Lasswell, politicians are generally individuals suffering from an inferiority complex. Lasswell summarized his theory in a formula: p}d} r = P, where p equals private motives, d equals displacement onto a public object, r equals rationalization in terms of public interest, and P equals the political man (Lasswell 1930:75). In Lasswell's model, it is the personal that becomes the political. According to Lasswell, politicians have an intense and unmet thirst for respect. To compensate for their low self-esteem, they seek power.

Lasswell's interest in psychodynamic processes led to his becoming one of the founders of political psychology as a separate research discipline. He borrowed ideas from the doyen of psychoanalysis, Sigmund Freud, who also evinced interest in people in the political world—US president Woodrow Wilson in particular. In collaboration with American diplomat William C. Bullit, Freud sought to explain Wilson's failure at the 1919 peace talks in Versailles and his later inability to bring the United States into the fold of the League of Nations. In due course, the analysis raised an outcry.[1] Freud determined that a contributory cause of the failure was

Wilson's complex personality, partly because "his Ego had not achieved a satisfactory solution of the Oedipus complex" (Freud and Bullit 1999:51).[2]

From the ideas inspired by Harold Laswell that politicians' behavior is governed by factors rooted in psychodynamic processes, researchers eventually turned their attention to the circumstances of politicians' lives as well. It was, after all, difficult to empirically determine the relationship between politicians' psychological dispositions and their behavior (Immelman 2003). Consequently, there was a reorientation from how agents influence their worlds to how their worlds influence agents. And thus was the door opened to sociological explanatory models.

The key concepts were learned roles and contextual explanations. The personal ambitions of individuals were understood as subordinate to greater social contexts. Politics was analyzed from the macro perspective and understood as a product of social norms. The political system was thought to be structured to preserve and defend the prevailing order (Searing 1991). Various sociological studies produced a sea of information about the socioeconomic backgrounds of members of Congress (Davidsson 1969; Matthews 1954, 1960; Prewitt 1970; Wahlke et al. 1962), but less about how parliamentarians reasoned in an attempt to orient themselves in the political world.

As the sociological explanatory models celebrated triumphs, progress was unfolding in party research. When Anthony Downs published *An Economic Theory of Democracy* in 1957, it was a revelation for many political scientists, who began to understand politics in a completely different way. Downs's premise was that political parties are rational actors in an electoral market place. For the parties, the main goal is winning as many votes as possible. The "theory of relativity" of party research had seen the light of day. Using a few simple assumptions, we could understand contexts previously thought to be much more complex. Sociology was obliged to retreat, and in the latter half of the 1970s, the emphasis was on the individual.

The breakthrough of the rational choice model, and not psychological advances, was the primary reason for the change of perspective. By the mid-1980s, Kenneth A. Shepsle stated that (American) legislative scholars were a unique cadre among political scientists, where there were no schisms regarding how the activities of legislators should be understood: "the legislature as an arena in which self-interested behavior is manifested" (1985:12). Shane Martin made a similar observation some twenty years later. Martin argued that how we look at legislators as goal-oriented is "an almost unquestioned assumption in American scholarship" (2008:558).

Schematically, one can thus say that studies of and related to politicians' behavior have shifted focus over the years—from Harold Lasswell and the emphasis on psychological explanations, to the opposite point of view that assigns greater weight to social circumstances, and then onward to the current perspective, where politicians are regarded as rational actors governed by self-interest. The three theories approach career ambition differently. Lasswell saw ambition as a result of personal shortcomings among certain individuals, and their way to deal with these issues was to attain power. In more sociologically oriented research, ambition may instead be understood on the basis of external expectations and the institution's need for leaders (see, e.g., Bell and Price 1969; Davidson 1969; Kornberg 1967; Sorauf 1963; Wahlke et al. 1962). In such analyses, it becomes important to find out what types of roles exist in the parliament and what their functions are. The point of departure for the rational choice perspective is that individuals have latent career ambitions. The only question is, under what circumstances is a politician willing to pursue advancement? (see, e.g., Black 1972). The fundamental premise that politicians are self-interested actors driven by personal ambition came in the wake of Anthony Downs's arguments about vote-maximizing parties. It made sense to presume that utility-maximizing parties were made up of utility-maximizing individuals.

Some scholars go so far as to argue that it was the focus on political ambition that cleared the ground for the breakthrough of the rational choice model in the study of legislators' behavior. The dean of this school of thought, whom I will discuss soon—Joseph Schlesinger—took center stage. "This emphasis on individual ambition later made Schlesinger the patron saint of the rational choice theorists" (Fowler 1993:56).[3]

THE LACK OF STUDIES ON POLITICAL MOTIVATIONS IN THE EUROPEAN CONTEXT

There are significant differences between American and European research on this subject. Whereas American scholars have come to focus almost exclusively on what motivates individual agents, European research has long maintained its view of politicians as subordinate to institutional norms and structures. When Jens Borchert described German research, he emphasized the diverging points of departure "The very concept of self-interested legislators is anathema to this line of research" (2003:11). Borchert argued that Germany is not unique in Europe but may be the country that provides the most distinct contrast to American research. One illustrative Swedish example is a recent book that traces formations of government in Sweden between 1917 and 2009 (Hermansson et al. 2010). The book disregards the question of whether the people who sat in these governments may have pursued their positions. The authors were instead interested in the criteria used to select the various cabinet ministers. From this perspective, the personal motivations of cabinet ministers become irrelevant to understanding the formation of a government.

In a review article that discusses comparative legislative research in Europe, the author concluded, "There has been little research in Europe on what constitutes a 'political personality,' on ambition, on the motivation for entering politics, and on the risks of political careers. We have also little research comparing successful with unsuccessful candidates" (Patzelt 1999:259). Although Patzelt's determination was made some years ago, his conclusions still largely apply. Twelve years later, political scientists Jens Borchert and Klaus Stolz delivered a similar analysis: "The importance of political careers for the functioning and the development of multilevel systems of government and governance contrasts starkly with the scarce notice given to the topic in academic literature. The impact of political careers for interinstitutional linkage and members' behavior has hardly been studied—neither from a political careers nor from an institutionalist perspective" (2011:108).[4]

In other words, European political scientists have evinced no interest in political career ambition. Taken together, there is a fundamental difference between how American and European scholars have understood and studied politicians. In the next section I will discuss Joseph Schlesinger, the pioneer of studies about career ambition and politics and whose research is helpful also for studies of party-centered systems.

SCHLESINGER'S THEORY OF POLITICAL AMBITIONS

The first person to systematically investigate the role of ambition in politics was Joseph Schlesinger. His book *Ambition and Politics: Political Careers in the United States* was published in 1966. From the outset, in the introduction to the book, Schlesinger decreed, "Ambition is the heart of politics" (1966:1). Despite the pivotal importance of ambition, according to Schlesinger, scant regard is given to politicians' personal ambitions in research on their behavior. Schlesinger argued that the hopes of the intellectual that politicians are motivated solely by ideology or principle have little basis in reality.[5] Popular descriptions of elected representatives as self-interested are, however, rooted in proven experience. People in general clearly understand that politicians are seeking personal success. Schlesinger sharpened his argument by referring to a politician who carried the banner of egalitarianism. "Lenin was no more willing to delay his accession to power for the perfect Marxist revolution than is the office seeker in the United States who polls the voters for policy positions to insure his election" (1994:34).

In his work, Schlesinger aimed to survey the American political system based on the assumption that a politician's future career path can be predicted by observing the office he or she currently holds. Certain positions are springboards, and others are not. Three types of ambition are discussed in Schlesinger's study: progressive, static, and discrete (ibid., 33ff). Progressive ambitions refer to the office holder's aspirations to an office more important than the one now held or sought. Individuals with progressive ambitions thus want to rise in the political hierarchy. When ambition is static, the politician seeks to make a long-term career out of a particular office, whereas a politician with discrete ambition only wants a particular office for its set term and then chooses to withdraw.

Regardless of which type of ambition a politician had, Schlesinger assumed that their behavior was rational in relation to the office they were seeking. "[T]he most reasonable assumption is that ambition for office, like most other ambitions, arises within a specific situation" (ibid., 38). This implies that the ambition for office is "a response to the possibilities which lie before the politician" (ibid). The ingredients of Schlesinger's ambition theory are found in the confluence of structural conditions, politicians' personal ambitions, and competition for the office. He did not, however, preclude the existence of politicians who are indifferent to their chances and run for office in elections they know they cannot win. This may seem problematic for the theory, because it is based on the premise that politicians are rational actors who run only in elections they have a good chance of winning. The reason is primarily methodological.

The best way to study ambition is, according to Schlesinger, to observe which politicians run in which elections. These significant and clearly observable indicators become important in defining the various types of ambition. By studying in which elections politicians run for office, one can study politicians' estimations of their own career opportunities (ibid., 38–39).

Based on the theory, a politician who does not run for office has discrete ambition. The person who runs for reelection is assigned a static ambition. A member of the US House of Representatives who runs for the Senate is expressing progressive ambition. It is the mapping of these possibilities upon which Schlesinger's actual work based. Schlesinger did not precisely establish the nature of the relationship between offices and ambitions; it remains unclear whether offices attract ambitious politicians or whether certain offices elicit—or compel—a particular type of ambition. Schlesinger argued that this has no significant impact on his study, since the research interest has to do with the American career system as such (ibid., 38).

IN THE WAKE OF JOSEPH SCHLESINGER

Joseph Schlesinger's typology of ambition has inspired many political scientists, particularly in the United States. The assumption that contextual circumstances are important has gained support over the years. Scholars have shown that US states with strong party organizations produce more experienced candidates (Haeberle 1985; Kunkel 1988; Mezey 1970). There is also evidence that candidates from states with more professionalized legislatures are more likely to win open-seat elections (Robeck 1982). For his part, Schlesinger (1985) found that when the Republicans increased their constituencies in the American South, competition became fiercer and the number of previously uncontested seats declined.

Even though Schlesinger assigned weight to the contextual factors, the main focus was on the agent. In the wake of Schlesinger, individual candidates' estimations and calculations concerning their future careers have been accorded considerable attention (Abramson, Aldrich, and Rohde 1987; Banks and Kiewiet 1989; Black 1972; Brace 1984; Kazee 1994; Levine and Hyde 1977; Moncrief, Squire, and Jewell 2001; Rhode 1979; Stone and Maisel 2003). Many of the studies have presumed that all politicians have progressive ambitions to achieve higher offices. This seeking of higher office is affected by the opportunities available and what the politician expects to win or lose. One of the first to create such a cost/benefit model was Gordon Black (1972),[6] who used his model to show that the political system plays a role in determining the inflow of ambitious individuals. Black argued that the political system does not cause ambition but acts as a filter that allows some types of individuals through, while others are stopped (ibid., 158). The structure of the political system, according to Black, affects both which politicians succeed in the fray and which politicians run for office. David Rhode (1979) expanded on Black's model and gave it a clearer theoretical framework, in which a fundamental assumption is that members of the House of Representatives have progressive ambitions.

With the assumption that all members possess progressive ambitions, various calculations have been designed to predict when a politician will run for office (see, e.g., Brace 1984; Codispoti 1982; Kazee 1994; Moncrief, Squire, and Jewell 2001; Stone and Maisel 2003). Less research has been done to study the consequences of progressive ambitions on how things play out in the legislative assemblies (Treul 2009).

Research on career ambition has also taken on a feminist approach. Women have difficulty advancing in American politics; they are systematically underrepresented in the legislative assemblies. Despite this, when women do run for office they are as successful as men when it comes to fundraising and winning elections (Carroll 1994; Fox 2000). And once inside the legislative assemblies, there are no gender differences in men's and women's abilities to get legislation passed (Bratton and Haynie 1999).[7] Based on these aspects, there should be no reason for women to refrain from running for office (for a review of this field of research, see Lawless and Fox 2010; Lawless and Pearson 2008), but the research shows that individual motivation and expectations are highly significant to who runs for office. Women often underestimate their own ability and do not see themselves as sufficiently competent candidates for office (Lawless and Fox 2005).[8]

CRITICISM OF AMBITION THEORY

Schlesinger and scholars who have applied his theory have been the object of criticism from various angles. The objections fall mainly into two camps. The first category of criticism comes from "the inside," and its thrust is that the division into three categories of ambition should actually be expanded. John Hibbing argued that scholars who have applied Schlesinger's typology have overlooked the fact that static ambition need not be "static." That a member runs for reelection (to the House of Representatives, for example) does not necessarily mean the member would turn down other high-status positions. The member may seek positions within an institution, such as a committee chairmanship or the position of party whip (Hibbing 1986). One should, according to Hibbing, therefore differentiate between members who only want to be reelected and those who want to advance in positions within an institution. Hibbing designated the latter type of ambition *intrainstitutional*. Subsequent research has paid little heed to this criticism, but the studies that have been done nevertheless indicate that intrainstitutional ambition exists and that it differs from static and progressive ambition (Herrick and Moore 1993).

The second category of criticism has to do with how political ambition is measured. Linda Fowler, for example, pointed out that Schlesinger assumed the existence of politically ambitious people and did not explore the circumstances under which political ambitions arise. Fowler argued that Schlesinger's theory is therefore not a theory of ambition but a theory of political careers (Fowler 1993:57). Rebekah Herrick also examined (2001) how her colleagues studied ambition. Herrick argued that unless ambition is recognized as a psychological phenomenon, the research may be unreliable. Because scholars have not taken this into account, according to Herrick, they have mainly studied which politicians run for a particular office and which do not, without having ascertained that the choice is a matter of ambition.

In turn, this has implications for how the effect of ambition on members' behavior in the legislatures should be interpreted. This is a cart-before-the-horse problem: to explain politicians' behavior (their career ambitions) is something that comes *after* that which is to be explained (ibid., 470). In other words, the indicator of ambition is the seeking of higher office, but the candidacy comes after the member has served in the legislature for a number of years. Thus, the behavior itself may have created the conditions for a member to run for higher office, which stands in contrast to the assumption that it was the ambition that influenced the behavior.

In response, Herrick made an attempt to more closely examine the effects of political ambition on the behavior of members of Congress. She used surveys to study non-incumbent candidates running in the 1992–1994 House elections. Slightly fewer than half the winning candidates responded, 89 all told. The freshmen representatives were asked about their future ambitions and rated the strength of their wishes for a particular position on a scale of one to five. They had three positions to choose among: party leader, committee chair in the House of Representatives, and a seat in the US Senate (ibid., 470ff.) Thereafter, Herrick tracked the respondents' legislative activity in Congress (bill introductions and floor activity—participation in debates, etc.).

The findings indicated that earlier research may have overestimated the effects of political ambition on legislative behavior. The conclusions of the study were cautious, however, due to the limited sample size: "ambition's effects on behavior may be stronger than the relationships detected here but weaker than those detected elsewhere" (ibid., 473). As Herrick only studied freshmen representatives of the House, it's unclear to what extent the findings say something about the ambitions of newcomers versus about political ambition in general. Members who have learned the rules of the game may modify their behavior, even if the ambition remains the same. In addition, Herrick's conclusions about the effects of political ambition may be exaggerated due to erroneous assumptions.

Even though Herrick presented relatively strong criticism and important objections to how the mainstream has studied political ambition, her colleagues paid little heed. Research on and surrounding political ambition in members of Congress is still moving along the same lines (see, e.g., Treul 2009). In this context, it should be noted that one logical explanation for why more scholars have not taken Herrick's arguments to heart has to do with the inauspicious conditions. Members of the US Congress are not particularly accommodating about answering research surveys.[9] Scholars interested in political career ambition are thus compelled to adjust their data collection to the inability to get information from the members themselves. As a result, American scholars find it difficult to make any pronouncements about how many representatives have long-term and goal-oriented ambitions to climb the political career ladder and to differentiate them from other members who have discrete ambitions and run for office in a single election.

APPROACHES TO STUDYING POLITICAL
CAREER AMBITION

It may—setting aside Rebekah Herrick's criticism—be thought reasonable to assume that politicians who run for office have some kind of career ambition. Likewise, there are actually politicians who run for office without really wanting the job. In a study that included Norwegian local politicians, Jacob Aars and Audun Offerdal (1998) showed that this does occur.[10] The study participants—candidates on the ballot for a municipal election—were asked why they had agreed to run. Two-thirds of the nominees reported that they agreed to run because their chances of being elected were slim (ibid., 214). Ambition and candidacy are thus not necessarily synonymous. Ambitious politicians may also avoid running for office because the competition is too fierce or because the conditions are not right for other reasons (Woodward 1996).

An alternative way to study career ambition would thus be to more closely examine the politicians who have successfully attained influential positions. The connection between the desire for career attainment and later achieving it may seem very close, but things are not really that simple. An ambitious politician may encounter resistance and be outstripped by someone whom the party believed more suitable, even though that someone had not sought the position.

In his memoirs, former Swedish prime minister Tage Erlander related how things went when he accepted the office of party leader: "I am afraid, have always been afraid, and the reason I am accepting now is truly not because I am enterprising and want power, but rather fear of the group" (Erlander 2001:142). There was someone else, however, who did want the job—but the party leadership did not want Gustav Möller. This illustrates how the relationship between career ambition and the actual outcome can be complex.[11]

Another alternative would be to interview MPs. The prerequisites for attaining personal ambitions could be discussed in an interview and, based on the answers, conclusions drawn about the MPs' motives for pursuing a political career. This would naturally be dependent upon the MPs' willingness to talk about their experiences. There is reason to believe that it is easier to talk about the issue of personal ambition if there is a statistical basis for the conversation. Other researchers have found that when asked delicate questions, MPs can find it difficult to "discern the pattern when personally caught up in an activity" (Wängnerud 1998:54). Survey studies have proved to be a successful method when the intent is to study people's experiences concerning delicate subjects (Aquilino 1994; Turner, Miller, and Moses 1990, chapter 6; Turner, Lessler, and Devore 1992). Sampling alternatives are another advantage of survey studies. It is difficult to achieve a total sample of all members of parliament, but more than 90 percent of MPs are included in the parliamentary study used for this book.

In general, one can say that different approaches present different challenges. The challenge in this case is whether it is possible, based on survey questions, to bring any clarity to the matter of political ambition among Swedish MPs and the consequences.

DEFINING POLITICAL CAREER AMBITION

As we embark upon this study of career ambition in the Swedish parliament, there is good reason to think about what actually distinguishes an ambitious politician. Influential philosophers such as Plato, Aristotle, Seneca, Thomas Aquinas, Niccolo Machiavelli, John Locke, Jean-Jacques Rousseau, and Adam Smith have all discussed the distinctive traits of ambitious individuals. A great deal of thought has thus been devoted to this and related phenomena, which may be interesting to explore.

Philosopher Glen Pettigrove has argued that the deliberations of the influential philosophers have seldom received any extensive analysis, which Pettigrove found remarkable considering that office ambition plays a significant role in Western politics (Pettigrove 2007:54). In response, he attached philosophical arguments to a number of criteria that distinguish personal career ambition (ibid.). This synthesis also forms the basis of the criteria that will be used to study MPs' career ambitions in this book.

Pettigrove began his argument by asking whether ambition is a virtue or a vice. There is no obvious answer to this question. Certainly, Aquinas, Machiavelli, Locke, and others have regarded ambition as a threat to a nation's political security (ibid.), but Pettigrove rhetorically mused whether it would be reasonable to fault Nelson Mandela for desiring greater political power as he languished in prison (ibid., 59). Thus, whether ambition is good or bad cannot form the basis of the actual standard, according to Pettigrove.

The main issue is, rather, whether someone has an ambition. Pettigrove suggested Alexis de Tocqueville as the philosopher who has come closest to defining the central issue. Tocqueville held that ambition is the longing for advancement, with focus on "a yearning desire to rise." But the lust for success is not the be-all and end-all. In his synthesis of the distinguishing characteristics of ambition, Pettigrove listed the following criteria:

Ambition involves a self-disciplined commitment or determination to obtain its object. Otherwise, it is merely a pipe dream or a formless, general wish.

The commitment and desire of ambition must manifest themselves in actions. Taking action is critical to obtaining the desired end. Even if an individual's desires are intense, writing something down on a wish list is not enough. Ambitious people take action to attain their objectives.

Ambition's end cannot be achieved overnight. There must be a plan of action. Fighting for a particular end one day and then fighting equally hard for something else the next is not a characteristic of the ambitious person.

The end toward which ambition's desire and commitment are directed is difficult to achieve. Pettigrove admitted that specifying the nature of the difficulty surrounding the object of ambition is not always easy. So what actually separates an ambitious person from a less ambitious person? Pettigrove suggested that it is the difference between a prince who would one day be king and an ordinary citizen with the same aspirations. The former individual is thus less ambitious than the latter. Pettigrove maintained that there should also be an element of realism in the ambition. A person who aspires to a position should have the ability to obtain it. If someone fervently wants something and does everything in his or her power to achieve it but lacks the prerequisites/talent for doing so, the ambition becomes something else entirely.[12]

We can begin to grasp the true nature of ambition based on the philosophers' reasoning. Ambition involves taking a long-term approach to the work of improving one's current position. The individual must also take actions to achieve the position. The position must be realistic but not especially easy to attain. The ambition to make a successful career in politics is thus not a game of chance but a goal-oriented enterprise that continues over time.

I would, however, like to add a fifth criterion to the other four while incorporating the empirical research. Empirical research has a criterion that elected representatives with progressive ambitions endeavor to replace their current institutions with others of higher status. We can thus use empirical research to both more clearly define and flesh out the philosophical argument that the object of an ambition must be difficult and probable by adding that the MP must want to leave the parliamentary office for a position in another institution of higher status.[13]

The definition of career ambition that will be used in this book thus involves striving to climb the career ladder. My interest is directed at politicians who take a long-term approach to their efforts to improve their current position. We will leave the question of *why* someone might want to improve their position for another day. The motive is thus not the main thing—our focus is instead on the actual ambition to achieve a successful personal career. This implies that the definition may apply to politicians who want to make a political career for different reasons. At the outset, their least common denominator is that they are seeking career advancement. The point of departure is that there may be politicians with career ambitions, just as there may be those who have none.

THE ROAD AHEAD

The structure of the book harkens back to some extent to Herrick's work, but unlike Herrick's study the analysis undertaken here will be more elaborated in two respects. First, I will study whether the MPs who have plans for the future meet the criteria to be categorized as politicians with personal career ambitions—that is, ambitious politicians. This type of validation is novel in this field of research. Second, the Swedish MPs will, more so than in the American research, also appear as individuals and not only utility-maximizing actors. The Swedish MPs are asked about their views on the representative office and what strategic choices they have made to give them the capacity to exert influence. I will also more closely examine the relationship between *wanting* to achieve career attainment and actually *doing* so. All of this is, of course, provided that Swedish MPs with career ambitions exist—and are willing to admit it. We will begin looking for the answer to this question in the next chapter.

3. Are There MPs Who Aspire to High Positions?

We will now turn to the question of whether there are MPs in the parliament who are working long-term to achieve a successful political career. The process here is intended as an initial validation of the Parliamentary Study data presented in Chapter 1.

THE EMPIRICAL INDICATOR

The survey question upon which the book is based was taken from the 1996 Parliamentary Study, in which MPs were queried about their interest in various political positions. The question read, "Where would you like to see yourself in ten years? (You may tick more than one box)." The MPs could select from eleven options:

- Member of the parliament
- Party group leader in the parliament
- Chair of a parliamentary committee
- Chair of a nationwide organization/association
- Cabinet minister in the Swedish government
- Member of the European Parliament
- Political group leader in the European Parliament
- Chair of a European Parliament committee
- Chair of a European organization/association
- EU commissioner
- Withdrawn from public life

This survey question will serve as the empirical indicator of the MPs' career ambitions. The question must be validated in order to confirm that the question has truly identified MPs who are pursuing a long-term political career.

The validation applies if the survey material can be used to reflect the MPs' personal ambitions as a genuine phenomenon. The question is whether we are using the survey question to study the MPs' career ambitions—or something else altogether.

It is by no means established that there are MPs who are working deliberately and over the long term in an attempt to attain the highest positions. An alternative scenario is that the MPs are simply carrying on and not devoting any significant energy to planning their own careers. When we listen to high-ranking Swedish politicians, they seem to describe their political careers precisely thus, which may indicate that there are no ambitious politicians in the Swedish parliament. It might also be so that MPs conceal their aspirations due to the negative connotations of ambition. The political memoir literature shows that MPs striving to achieve a successful career in politics have a price to pay. We have looked at accounts that establish rather clearly that career ambition is hardly saluted in the Swedish context. In a party-centric system, personal political ambition may indeed be at work, but "under the radar." We will bring these considerations along as we set about answering the main question of this chapter: Are there politicians in the Swedish parliament who state that they want prominent positions in answer to a direct question from researchers in a survey?

THE THEORETICAL DEFINITION AND THE SURVEY QUESTION

The criteria that constitute the theoretical definition of political ambition were discussed in Chapter 2. The criteria are that the ambitious MP must have a *long-term approach* and must want to *move* to an institution with *higher* status. The object of ambition must be *difficult* to obtain, and the MP must be *committed* and *acting* to attain the object. Each of the criteria must now be related to how the survey question is designed. The review applies to all criteria except action.

Action has its own chapter (Chapter 5) and does not have the same initial significance. To make the study of MPs' behavior interesting, we must first confirm the existence of MPs who report that they want more prominent positions.

Long-Term Approach

One of the criteria that apply to career ambition is that the MP is working long-term toward attaining the object. This does not, so to speak, involve a game of chance; the MP must be working toward something over time. When a person is asked whether he or she wants to be prime minister, a cabinet minister, party leader, and so on and answers "yes," this is not, according to the arguments of the classical philosophers, an absolute indication of ambition. This kind of question instead has to do with whether the person is willing to accept an office or a position in general. Those who are ambitious must be willing not only to subject themselves to the hard work that the position demands, but also struggle in the hopes of one day being able to shoulder the role of minister, party leader, and the like. Long-term career ambition should thus be regarded not as an invitation to partake of a smorgasbord of positions but rather as preparation for taking a seat at the table.

If this line of argument is extended to the survey question, it involves the MPs' aspirations for the next ten years. A decade is an eternity in politics. The individual MP must survive both general elections and internal party nominations. The temporal aspect of the survey question is thus important, because it is included as a cost for attaining the object and implies that the MP has made a long-term commitment.

The MP Must Be Willing to Move to a Higher-Status Institution

In American research, the operationalization of ambition has been based on the intentions of ambitious members to replace their current position (in one institution) with a position in another institution of higher status. Based on such a criterion, the survey question must include positions in institutions with higher status than the office of MP. The options the MPs were asked to consider in 1996 included "Cabinet minister in the Swedish government," for example, as well as various positions within the EU organization. The structure of the question thus makes it possible to identify offices/positions that meet the criterion that the MP must want to move to an institution with higher status. Based on this criterion, the position of cabinet minister and the various EU positions will be included in the operationalization of career ambition.

The reason positions in the EU parliament are included in the operationalization is that earlier research has shown that the EU parliament enjoys a certain status among Swedish parliamentarians (Hagevi 2003). The study applied to MPs in office during the 1994–1998 term. In the 1994 Parliamentary Study, MPs were given the opportunity to rank various political positions on a scale of 0–10. A seat in the EU parliament came in seventh, with a mean score of 7, whereas a seat on a parliamentary committee came in fourteenth, with a mean score of 4.3 (ibid., 363). The EU parliament had higher status than the office of county governor or the position of director-general of a government agency. Cabinet minister was the position that topped the status list. The office of EU commissioner was ranked second, with a mean score of 8.9. At that point in time, Swedish parliamentarians thus ranked the EU parliament relatively highly and believed it had higher status than a seat in the parliament.

Based on the Schlesinger typology, I would have to mix different types of ambitions were I to include two other positions, party whip and committee chair, in the operationalization. Research in this field has followed Schlesinger's lead, and when politicians with progressive ambitions are studied, it is presumed that they want to leave their current institution for one with higher status (see Chapter 2). An MP who reports that he or she wants to advance in the parliament but not serve in the cabinet or move to Brussels would, according to Schlesinger's theoretical assumptions, be the holder of a static ambition and would not have any progressive ambitions as defined by Schlesinger.

The Object of Ambition Must Be Difficult

In her memoirs, former cabinet minister Ulla Lindström wrote, "A career in politics can start anywhere. But the cabinet is the final destination" (1970:129). Obviously, the opportunity to reach this final destination is not granted to everyone.[1] Over the years, the proportion of parliamentarians who have been appointed to positions in the Swedish cabinet has declined (Bäck et al. 2007). In the 1994 election the Social Democrats won 161 seats and the government administration was made up of 22 ministers. About 60 percent of the ministers had been members of parliament at some time, which implies that just over 8 percent of the Social Democratic MPs in the parliament may be considered for a ministerial post. It should be noted that MPs cannot openly campaign for a ministerial position; the appointments are made by a small circle of people who must consider a wide range of factors including gender, constituency, and competence. Nor has it been easy for central-right MPs to achieve positions in the cabinet over the years, but for reasons that are easy to understand, that is even truer for MPs from the Green Party and Left Party. We therefore have solid grounds for establishing that cabinet positions meet the criterion that the effort must apply to something difficult to achieve.

It is less certain how the difficulty of becoming a member of the EU parliament (MEP) should be assessed. In 1996 when the question was asked, Sweden had 22 seats to allocate among the parties. Unlike ministerial positions, most of the individuals who become MEPs are selected from MPs in the Riksdag. Accordingly, it is probably easier to rise to the EU parliament than to capture a ministerial post. This is counterbalanced by the fact that the survey question also includes positions within the EU organization that are very difficult for a Swedish MP to attain, such as EU commissioner and party coordinator on a committee; accordingly, the various EU positions still qualify as *difficult*.[2]

The MP Must Be Committed

The fourth criterion has to do with *commitment*. An MP must be committed to his or her aspirations for the future. Commitment is closely related to having a long-term approach. In this case, a long-term approach refers to the fact that the political positions/offices are not immediate prospects. The question thus becomes whether the MPs are committed to attaining the more prominent positions even if they have been members of the parliament for more than one term. The seniority principle, for example, might inhibit MPs' ambitions if they perceive that only long and faithful service is rewarded.

To answer this question we must compare MPs recently elected for the first time and MPs who have sat in parliament for quite some time. My intention here is to preclude the possibility that we are dealing *with a first-termer phenomenon:* a situation in which it is primarily first-term members who want the more prominent positions. If there is a clear division between MPs in terms of overrepresentation of the first-termer group, it would indicate that we are not dealing with committed MPs. The MPs' political career aspirations would in such case be interpreted to mean that such interest soon fades and that the MPs are not particularly committed. If, however, there are no significant differences between first-term MPs and other MPs, it would signal commitment among the MPs. To put it another way: after only a few years in the parliament, the "tooth of time" should not have gnawed away at MPs' political career ambitions. Before we can test the MPs' commitment, we must first find out whether there are any MPs who report that they are interested in more prominent positions.

MPS AND PROMINENT POSITIONS

Table 3.1 shows the results from the survey question about the MPs' aspirations for the next ten years. The MPs were asked to take a position on a number of fixed alternatives that had to do with their own futures. Because they were permitted to select more than one option, the table therefore does not add up to 100.

The table shows that 21 percent of MPs may be interested in the positions covered by the definition of career ambition—cabinet minister and positions in an EU organization. The largest proportion, 14 percent, aspires to a cabinet position. Slightly fewer are aiming for a career in Brussels. We can also see that the position of parliament committee chair is as desirable as a cabinet position in government.

The two most popular options, however—"withdrawn from public life" and "MP in the parliament"—are unrelated to ambition. The most important observation for my purposes is that there is a group of MPs who say they would like to be a cabinet minister and/or move work for the European parliament. Accordingly, at least some MPs have reported an interest in the more prominent positions.

Because the MPs were allowed to select more than one option in the survey, we cannot confirm that the proportion of MPs who want to move on to a higher-

Table 3.1 Future plans of Swedish MPs (%)

National level	
Withdrawn from public life	65
MP in the parliament	23
Party group leader in the parliament	3
Chair of parliament committee	14
Cabinet minister in the Swedish government	14
Chair of nationwide organization/association	7
European level	
Member of the European Parliament	4
Political group leader, European Parliament	0
Chair of EU parliament committee	1
EU commissioner	2
Chair of European organization/association	0
Number of persons	281

Source: Parliamentary Study 1996.
Note: The survey question read, "Where would you like to be ten years from now? (You may select more than one position)."

status institution is 21 percent. To arrive at the correct proportion, we must determine whether there are MPs in this group interested in more than one position within the EU organization and/or the position of cabinet minister. For this reason, the career variable that will be used throughout the book is presented in Table 3.2.

Of the 281 MPs who answered the question, 18 percent indicate that they want to progress from the parliament. This implies that 18 percent of MPs in the parliament may potentially be categorized as ambitious. The 21 percent shown in the preceding table means that there were a number of MPs who were interested in more than one prominent position.

Table 3.1 shows that 14 percent of the MPs aspired to become a committee chair and 3 percent aspired to become the party group leader. In order to find out how many MPs are interested only in a career in the parliament, those who want to advance in the parliament are separated from those who also aspire to progress from the parliament; the results are shown in Table 3.3.

When the MPs interested in positions outside the parliament are separated

Table 3.2 Proportion of MPs who indicate ambition to move from the parliament to a higher-status institution

Yes	18%
Number of persons	281

Source: Parliamentary Study 1996.

Table 3.3 Proportion of MPs who indicate interest only in a career in the parliament

Yes	11%
Number of persons	281

Source: Parliamentary Study 1996.

from those whose ambitions are limited to positions inside parliament, it emerges that 11 percent of the MPs aspire to be a committee chair and/or party group leader, but otherwise not advance upward in the political system. In other words, there are more MPs who want to advance outside the parliament than MPs who want to advance inside parliament. In Chapter 7 I will take a closer look at whether 18 percent is a little or a lot by means of a comparison to other parliaments. It may also be interesting to relate these figures to those that emerged in earlier Parliamentary Studies.

The 1994 Parliamentary Study gave MPs the opportunity to state why they wanted to sit on a select committee. Of the respondents, 10 percent (30 MPs) said they would like to sit on a select committee for the power and prestige (Hagevi 1998). The *Representation from Above* study (Esaiasson and Holmberg 1996) discussed MPs' "political ambition." The authors' operationalization was based mainly on the MPs' aspirations to remain in the parliament for another term of office.[3] We can say that the distinction in this context was between the MPs who wanted to remain in the parliament and those who did not. In 1994, 65 percent of respondents reported that they wanted to be reelected.

In the 2002 Parliamentary Study, MPs were able to leave optional comments to a question about their plans for the future. The question read, "Presuming that you are reelected, do you want to continue serving as an MP over the next 5 to 10 years, or would you prefer to do something else?" Respondents could select one of two options. The first was, "Continue serving as an MP," and the other was, "Do something else." Because the MPs responding to the 2002 survey were less compelled to disclose their career ambitions than they were in the 1996 survey, I chose to more closely study what the MPs had to say under such conditions. (Which also begs the question of the possible emotional connotations associated with ambition and whether there is reason to suspect that the MPs chose for various reasons not to answer the question that concerns their own futures.)

Of the 327 MPs who responded to the 2002 survey, 59 chose to avail themselves of the opportunity to write a comment. Six replied that they want to progress in the political system—a scant 2 percent. It therefore appears that when MPs are given the option to remark on their future plans in a survey study, only a negligible proportion indicate that they have career ambitions. One possible conclusion from this is that MPs are not less inclined to talk about their career ambitions in response to a direct question than they are when afforded the opportunity to comment on their future plans in general.

Based on the discussion of the emotional connotations of ambition, we can also compare how many MPs answered the question about their future plans with the response frequency for other questions. Overall, 314 MPs responded to the 1996 Parliamentary Study. Of the total, 89 percent answered the question about their future plans; thus, there was internal dropout of 11 percent. Is this dropout big or small? There was another question in the 1996 Parliamentary Study that touched upon the MPs' future plans, but only for the next electoral term. Various positions were not specified; the MPs were instead asked whether they wanted to remain in politics at the national or European level, do something else, or withdraw after the next electoral term. The response rate to this question was 92 percent. The difference in response tendency between the questions is thus insignificant. When other questions are asked about subjects that can be said to concern more personal matters, such as religious affiliation and marital status, the response frequency is somewhat higher, at just above 96 percent. Nonetheless, no significant reluctance to answer the question about future plans can be discerned.

We can also look at this argument from another perspective. The list of positions could possibly awaken the MPs' aspirations. On the survey questionnaire, the general question about the MPs' future plans for the next electoral term comes immediately before the question about the next ten years. This provides an opportunity to compare whether some of the MPs who said they wanted to leave politics changed their minds when they were given various types of political positions to choose among. But no such effect is found. Only one MP who wanted to leave changed his/her mind when presented with the more specific question and instead reported an interest in the more prominent political positions.

Earlier in this chapter I emphasized that the survey question contains a temporal aspect of ten years, which implies that the positions will not simply be dropped into the MPs' laps. However, we cannot surmise whether the MPs have understood this cost. In order to determine whether the temporal aspect is significant, we once again compare the MPs' answers about what they intend to do during the next electoral term with their plans for the next ten years. What we are studying here is whether there is any difference between the percentage of MPs who want to stay in politics and those who want to leave depending on whether the temporal aspect is the next electoral term or a longer period of time. The indicator that the MPs have understood the temporal aspect is that there would be more MPs who want to leave politics in ten years than MPs who want to leave during the next electoral term.

The data presented in Table 3.4 imply that the MPs have taken the temporal

Table 3.4 Comparison of MPs who want to remain in politics for the next term in office and MPs who want to remain in politics for ten more years

Next term in office	81%
Another 10 years	40%
Difference	41%***
Number of persons	289

Source: Parliamentary Study 1996.

Note: The question was, "After your current term in office, would you prefer to remain in politics at the national level, prefer a political position at the EU level, or prefer something else?" Those who answered that they wanted to withdraw or preferred "another position" have been categorized as not wanting to remain for another term in the parliament. The categorization for whether they want to remain in the parliament for another ten years is based on answering "Withdrawn from public life" to the question "What would you like to be doing in 10 years?" *p < .10, ** p < .05, ***p < .01.

aspect into account. The majority, 81 percent, of MPs would like to stay in office for another term, whereas 40 percent of MPs want to remain in politics for ten more years.[4]

TESTING THE MPS' COMMITMENT

The point of departure for the empirical test was the discussion of the MPs' commitment, which had to do with whether their interest in prominent positions should be regarded as a first-term phenomenon. In order to examine the MPs' commitment, I divided them into two groups: those elected for the first time in 1994, and those who had been in office longer. What I want to know is whether the MPs' aspirations for high positions are a first-term phenomenon. For the MPs to be categorized as *committed* there must be no significant difference between the MPs depending on whether they were elected for the first time in 1994 or earlier. I also include in the analysis those MPs who indicated interest only in a career in the parliament in order to have a basis of comparison.

Table 3.5 shows that the group I am interested in, MPs who have ambitions beyond the parliament, is not divided in the same way as the MPs who are only interested in influential positions within the parliament.

The data show that 20 percent of the first-term MPs are found among those who aspire to influential positions inside and outside the parliament. The corresponding figure among those who have been in office for more than two years is 16 percent. The difference is not particularly large and is not significant. When the same division is done among MPs who are interested only in a career in the parlia-

Table 3.5 Comparison of experienced and first-term MPs with respect to their future plans

	Aspire to influential positions inside and outside the parliament (%)	Aspire to influential positions inside the parliament (%)
First term	20	18
Experienced	16	6
Difference	4	12***
Number of persons	281	281

Source: Parliamentary Study 1996.
Note: All MPs elected to the Swedish parliament for the 1994–1998 term are counted as first-term MPs. *$p < .10$, **$p < .05$, ***$p < .01$.

ment, it emerges that 18 percent of the first-term MPs aspire to career attainment in the parliament, but only 6 percent of the MPs in office for more than two years report that they want to advance within the parliament. The difference is both clear and statistically significant.[5]

Those who say they aspire to positions outside the parliament are thus more committed than MPs who say they only want to advance within the parliament. When the two career interests are tested in a regression analysis, there is a significant effect of the MPs' tenure in the parliament and whether the MPs' aspire to prominent parliamentary positions. The longer MPs have sat in the parliament, the less interested they are in prominent positions within this institution. The equivalent does not apply to MPs who aspire to positions outside the parliament. The number of terms MPs have sat in the parliament has no effect on ambitions to advance beyond the parliament. The differences reinforce the impression that the design of the empirical indicator may, at least in connection with these initial tests, have captured something that agrees with the criterion that to be categorized as ambitious, a politician must be committed.

POTENTIALLY AMBITIOUS MPS

I asked a simple question at the beginning of the chapter: Are there politicians in the parliament who report that they want more prominent positions? The answer is yes: 18 percent of the MPs seem to be interested in a sustained political career. It is still too early to definitively state that these politicians in fact have personal career ambitions. What we know is that almost one out of five members answered that they are interested in a number of prominent positions. According to the definition used in this book, to be categorized as an ambitious MP the member must be committed to long-term action to attain lofty objectives. The mere fact that a number of MPs ticked the box to indicate their aspirations to move to a higher-status institution thus does not suffice to confirm that ambition is a motivator in politics.

Although there is a great deal left to do before we can conclude that we are dealing with genuine ambition, we have nonetheless been able to see in this chapter that the survey question initially met the criteria that the classical philosophers require to identify someone as ambitious. We could also see that the survey question covers the requirement that the MPs must aspire to move to a higher-status institution. In order to make any more definitive statement about the role of ambition as a motivator in party politics, however, we need indicators in addition to the fact that 18 percent of MPs are ambitious. The task in the next chapter is to more carefully test whether these MPs meant anything by their reported interest in more prominent positions.

4. Which MPs Aspire to High Positions?

A number of MPs report that they would personally like to have more prominent political positions. At this stage of the study, we could say that these individuals are "potentially ambitious" MPs. In this chapter I will bring greater clarity to the question of whether there is any substance to the MPs' answers in order to assess the strength of this potential.

One way to discover whether the MPs meant something beyond that the position(s) seemed intriguing when they ticked the boxes next to the more prominent positions on the survey is to look for any systematic classification in the material. There is no clear-cut way to perform such a search or any particular way that is best. My approach to the problem is to ask if there are any common attributes among the potentially ambitious MPs. By *common attributes* I mean circumstances connected to factors earlier in the parliamentarians' lives. Expressed in statistical terminology, you might say that I am looking for determinants that make it possible to predict which MPs have potential career ambitions.

If a connection is found between potentially ambitious MPs and their previous experiences, it will be considered evidence that efforts to attain influential positions are related to more fundamental factors among the MPs and that the MPs who reported interest in future positions are expressing more than a passing fancy for a particular job. If we return to the model presented in Chapter 1 for how career ambition will be studied, ambition is regarded as a dependent variable in this part of the analysis.

CAREER AMBITION AND POLITICAL PARTICIPATION

The point of departure for this chapter is that ambition can be seen as a form of political participation—at a high political level. Studies of and surrounding political participation are in most cases undertaken at the citizen level and apply to which citizens are interested in or already participating in various political activities (voting, protesting, party membership, etc.; see, e.g., Verba, Schlozman, and Brady 1995). In this case, we are studying the interest of the political elite in participating at the highest political level.

So, which MPs aspire to the most prominent positions in our political system? What I want to know is whether we can take the insights gained into civil political participation in general and find corresponding patterns among citizens at the elite level—our members of parliament.

Civil political participation is closely correlated to socioeconomic conditions. The connection between political participation and socioeconomic status is one of the most stable political science has to offer and is a firmly established field of social science research. Studies that highlighted the relationship between social position and political participation had already been undertaken by early in the twentieth century (Siegfried 1913; Sorokin 1927; Tingsten 1937). Among current researchers preoccupied with political participation, pointing out the strong correlation between socioeconomic conditions and people who are politically engaged has become something of a truism: "If we look for natural laws in the social sciences, the positive correlation between citizens' social and economic position and their political participation comes immediately to mind" (Gilljam 2003:203). It is, in other words, more likely that a politically engaged person will be highly educated and work at a high-paying job than the opposite—a correlation that recurs regardless of which part of the world we are studying (Norris 1996).

One of the things research has been able to show thus far concerning career ambition and its prerequisites is that ambitious politicians are more likely to run in elections where they can avoid an incumbent opponent, and also in electoral districts with professional organizations and a constituency that favors their party (see, e.g., Black 1972; Eulau and Prewitt 1973; Kazee 1994; Moncrief, Squire, and Jewell 2001; Rohde 1979; Stone and Maisel 2003). From this perspective, politicians should primarily be understood as strategic actors whose ambitions are manifested under favorable circumstances.[1] In a world of self-interested and rational actors, ambition is merely an expression of when it is strategically right to make a play for career advancement.

My thinking, however, is that if there is a connection between the MPs' resources and ambitions, it would imply that the connection is affected by factors related to more than merely strategic decisions. This would in turn have repercussions on the validity of the survey. In the event that there is a pattern between prominent political positions and the MPs' underlying experiences, it would indicate that the survey question used in the study may encompass a phenomenon related to ambition. Such a conclusion is based on the relationship between a survey question that concerns MPs' future plans and one of the most robust theories in political science. If there is such a relationship, it would mean that we can feel some confidence that the MPs who demonstrated aspirations for advancement were expressing more than just a passing fancy.

I WANT, I CAN, I MAY

The inspiration for this chapter is taken from studies of political participation—in particular, one of the most highly regarded theories in the field: the Civic Voluntarism Model (CVM). The CVM was introduced by Sidney Verba, Kay Schlozman, and Henry Brady in *Voice and Equality* (1995). The model is intended to explain what makes the correlation between socioeconomic factors and political participation so strong. The research team argued that political participation is related to three main factors: resources, engagement (motivation), and recruitment.

The internal relationship is described as follows: people with ample resources are engaged in issues revolving around politics and have acquired various types of civic skills through their occupations. These highly developed skills make these people interesting to political recruiters, who invite them to participate in political activities. Or, to put it more bluntly—people who become politically active are those who want to, can, and are asked (ibid., 463ff).

The CVM offers a theoretical context that not only focuses attention on the MPs' socioeconomic positions but also provides a more precise explanation for why socioeconomic factors are so significant to political participation. The intent of this chapter is therefore to test whether the individuals who say they want to climb the political career ladder have more resources, are more engaged, and have been recruited for political positions to a greater extent than their colleagues.

Other causes perhaps can be related to MPs' career ambitions as well. According to rational choice theory, politicians make strategic choices (see, e.g., Carson 2005; Jacobson 1989; Lublin 1994; Squire 1989). One such strategic choice might be to join a specific political party. The parties are the central agents in parliaments. A great deal of the politicians' opinions and positions can be traced back to the party to which they belong. The question is whether the same applies to their ambitions. In this chapter, the political parties will constitute an explanation that complements the socioeconomic model. Two patterns are of particular interest, which we can call the *strategy pattern* and the *culture pattern*. Strategic MPs should choose to join a party that can bring them to the highest positions. The Social Democratic Party has enjoyed a unique position as the governing party since World War II. For those who aspire to scale the political heights the Social Democrats, at least in the mid-1990s, offered the best opportunities to make such positions available to the MPs. No other party even came close.

One alternative on the same theme is that large parties attract ambitious people to a greater extent than other parties. In general, large parties have more positions to divvy up and can also reserve the largest number of positions in the government offices. If party size has an effect, politicians aiming for prominent positions should be found in the parties that have the muscle to give them prominent positions, and we should be able to determine that ambition is a matter of strategic choice.

There may also be party differences that have nothing to do with size. Research on party cultures shows that prevailing norms and ideas differ among the parties with respect to matters related to the role of the MP (Barrling Hermansson 2004; Elazar 1966; Freeman 1986). Hypothetically, it might be so that parties that are more informed by an individualist culture have a greater proportion of ambitious MPs, because the party norms make it easier for MPs to more overtly relate to the possibility of personal career attainment and because this type of politician in turn does not risk being penalized as severely as in less individualistic parties. A party informed by collectivist norms, in contrast, should by the same reasoning have fewer ambitious MPs because personal commitment to career advancement violates the collectivist spirit of the party.

Katarina Barrling Hermansson has shown that individuals are given greater scope in Sweden's Liberal Party, Green Party, and Left Party than is the case among the other parties (2004:301). The Green Party gives individuals the greatest latitude of all; it is not only made up of "individualists, but also demonstrates a high degree of individuality" (ibid., 238). If there are distinct differences among the parties unrelated to their size, such a pattern could be attributable to different party cultures that attract potentially ambitious MPs or where party norms deter this type of politician from joining the party or from declaring their ambitions.

The chapter is divided into four sections. In the first section I study the correlation between the MPs' socioeconomic backgrounds and potential career ambitions. Thereafter, the components brought to the fore by the CVM will be put to use. I'll look at how potentially ambitious MPs stand in relation to what Verba, Schlozman, and Brady call resources, engagement, and recruitment. The third section reports the distribution of potentially ambitious MPs among the political parties. The final section concludes with a regression analysis, where I will clarify whether there are any statistically sound correlations between the MPs' prior experiences and their career ambitions.

SOCIOECONOMICS AND PERSONAL AMBITION

Following is an investigation into whether the MPs' gender, childhood circumstances, education, and age relate to career ambition. The background variables and their possible correlations to ambition are presented below.

Gender Differences

I mentioned in Chapter 2 that American studies in political science are increasingly preoccupied with the relationship between gender and ambition (Fox and Lawless 2010), mainly in response to the underrepresentation of women in legislatures. Researchers have been able to show that there are differences between male and female American citizens who possess ample resources with regard to their inclination to run for political office. Men are more interested than women (Fowler and McClure 1989; Fox, Lawless, and Feeley 2001; Lawless and Fox 2005, 2010). There are, however, no gender differences when it comes to readiness to participate in political activities (Verba, Schlozman, and Brady 1995).

Researchers in Sweden have found a difference between men and women with regard to willingness to accept political positions at the local level (Nielsen 2001:32). Men are more interested in such positions than are women (20 percent and 12 percent, respectively). The differences between women and men have remained at the same levels for two decades, even though the proportion of women politicians has increased markedly over the years.[2]

The resource model emphasizes the importance of civic skills. With this in mind, women in the parliament should be more ambitious than men, because the proportion of MPs with a university education in the parliament was 75 percent for women in 1996, but only 61 percent for men.[3]

Nevertheless, we know from experience that more men than women have devoted themselves to politics and held the most ministerial positions, although these positions have been relatively evenly divided between the sexes since 1994.[4] The MPs themselves say that the reason women have not made their careers in politics to the same extent as men is that women lack the right networks (Niklasson 2005:105ff). Women's lack of access to the right networks may have a constraining effect on their career ambitions; and in such a case, the fact that women are better educated is not particularly significant.

Childhood and Education

Voting turnout, political knowledge, and democratic values are strongly correlated to level of education (Shields and Goidel 1997; Verba, Schlozman, and Brady 1995; Wolfinger and Rosenstone 1980). Highly educated individuals have skills that are useful in politics. These skills could constitute a strong foundation for individuals who aspire to advance in the political system. A person's education is often connected to the childhood environment and the educational attainment of his or her parents (McLoyd 1998; Sirin 2005; White 1982). Individuals with ample resources often come from affluent homes.

In relation to political participation, there is research showing that people who are politically socialized in childhood have faith in their capacity to get involved and make a difference (Prewitt 1970; Verba, Shlozman, and Brady 1995). This applies regardless of family socioeconomic status or parental background (Flanigan and Zingale 2002; Gaddie 2004; Prewitt, Eulau, and Zisk 1966). There are no data in the Parliamentary Studies of 1994 and 1996 that can clarify whether the MPs' parents were politically active. The information that is available instead concerns the parents' occupations. Consequently, we cannot determine the extent to which potentially ambitious MPs come from politically active homes. If the results were to show a connection between the MPs' family backgrounds and their career ambitions, one conceivable explanation might be that MPs who come from more economically disadvantaged homes were compensated through political engagement in the home. At the same time, it would be thought-provoking if there were a connection between an affluent family background and potentially ambitious MPs. This would indicate that aspirations to attain the more prominent positions can be traced as far back as the MPs' childhoods.

Age

The most natural connection between MPs' socioeconomic conditions and ambition should be age. Research on political ambition and age is not extensive, but "A conventional wisdom [is] that the window of opportunity for advancement to major office was somewhere between the mid-thirties and early fifties" (Gaddie 2004:24). Studies examining willingness to run for office have shown that interest in holding a first political office declines at age fifty-five (ibid.). We can see a similar attitude among Swedish citizens who were asked about their interest in elected office (Nielsen 2001:35). If this finding can be extended to our study of ambitious politicians, individuals over the age of fifty-five should be less ambitious than their younger colleagues.

TESTING THE CORRELATION BETWEEN SOCIOECONOMIC STATUS AND CAREER AMBITION

The time has come for an initial review of whether the MPs' socioeconomic status correlates to their aspirations and, if so, how. Can any underlying patterns be discerned in relation to which MPs reported interest in the more prominent positions? Table 4.1 shows us that such is in fact the case.

The data in Table 4.1 support our theoretical expectations. The classic assump-

Table 4.1 MPs' potential career ambitions and socioeconomic status

	Potential career ambition (%)	Difference (%)	Number of persons
Gender			
Male	20		164
Female	15	5	117
Family background			
Blue collar	10		62
Small business owner/farmer	15		53
White collar	26	16***	108
Education			
Not university educated	11		93
University educated	22	11***	172
Age			
23–35	29		24
36–55	25		59
56–69	3	26***	108

Source: Parliamentary Study 1996.
Note: The difference is calculated by subtracting the lowest value for each of the socioeconomic factors from the highest value. Family background data are based on the father's occupation. Only the father's occupation was used due to the large internal dropout in relation to the mother's occupation (54 percent). Internal dropout for the father's occupation was 13 percent. *$p < .10$, **$p < .05$, ***$p < .01$.

tion on socioeconomic conditions and political participation also appears to give rise to well-known differences when it comes to potential career ambition among the political elite. MPs from blue-collar homes are not as interested in the more prominent positions as are MPs from white-collar homes. Similarly, we can see that university-educated MPs are more likely to report aspirations to advance in the political system than MPs who have not attended university. People age 56+ seem to have little interest to speak of in a continued political career. Men, however, are not significantly more interested in prominent positions than women.

The next step is to flesh out the classic socioeconomic model with the mechanisms introduced by Verba, Schlozman and Brady. I will study the relationships between potential career ambition and the MPs' resources, engagement, and the extent to which they have been recruited for positions within the party.

MPS' CAREER AMBITIONS AND RESOURCES

When Verba and his colleagues discussed citizens' resources, they divided the resources into three components: time, money, and civic skills (Verba, Schlozman, and Brady 1995:271f). Time and money are of minor interest in this study.[5] The population is made up of full-time politicians who are paid to act politically. My focus is instead on civic skills; based on Verba, Schlozman, and Brady's typology I have chosen to more closely examine the MPs' occupational backgrounds, prior experience in voluntary organizations and the church, and their language skills.

Occupational Background

Verba, Schlozman, and Brady categorized the workplace among resources because "[h]aving a job is, of course a necessary first step toward acquiring civic skills in the workplace, but the nature of the occupation is also important" (1995:314). The MP's chosen occupation is thus a resource, which seems reasonable when one considers that there are *professional politicians* among the MPs elected to the parliament. A professional politician is someone who has specialized in the political craft. Given that occupational history is a resource, professional politicians should be more interested in a political career than former blue-collar workers, for example. MPs who were upon election to the parliament full-time employees of their parties, employed by a public sector organization to perform political work, or employed by lobbying organizations were categorized as professional politicians.[6] In 1996, the proportion of professional politicians in the parliament was 37 percent: the largest occupational group in the parliament after white-collar workers (Hagevi 2003).

Voluntary Organizations and the Church

In their study, Verba, Schlozman, and Brady showed that prior experiences working in voluntary organizations and churches are important channels to political participation. Familiarity with participating in the civil society is fostered by activity in various types of organizations (1995:310). In church, citizens become accustomed to acting in the congregation and participating in contexts in which they are trained to organize activities (ibid., chapter 11). Although religion and the church do not have the same unquestioned place in Sweden as in the United States, Swedish election researchers have determined over the years that there is a clear and stable correlation between party selection and religiosity (Hagevi 2009; Holmberg and Oscarsson 2004:67ff). Esaiasson and Holmberg have also shown that there is some correlation between MPs' religiosity and powerful positions (1996:40). This may mean that individuals who are religiously observant or active in a voluntary association also have experiences that foster interest in a political career.

Language Skills

In the literature on political participation, language skills are usually put into the category of "political sophistication" (Luskin 1990). When Verba, Schlozman, and Brady discussed the respondents' language skills, they referred to familiarity with the dominant language of their own society, English. In this case, we are dealing with a political elite, which means we can set a higher standard. The 1994 Parliamentary Study asks MPs whether they can read foreign-language texts (English, French, and German). Accordingly, I will compare MPs' ability to read a foreign language and their potential career ambitions. Language skills may be regarded as an important resource for the individual member when, through any career ambitions that may exist, they are to represent Sweden.

AN INITIAL TEST OF THE RELATIONSHIP
BETWEEN CAREER AMBITION AND RESOURCES

The relationship between potential career ambition and the MPs' resources is illustrated in Table 4.2.

Verba, Schlozman, and Brady's resource model elicits differences, but in the expected direction in only two cases. Among the various occupations, the professional politician category contains the highest percentage of potentially ambitious MPs. The percentage of professional politicians with potential career ambitions is more than twice as high as MPs whose occupational background is in the white-collar or blue-collar category.

Remarkably, none of the MPs in the category of small business owner/farmer have any aspirations for the more prominent positions. One explanation might be that almost 70 percent of the MPs in the small business owner category are older than fifty-five. There appears to be a connection between language skills and the MPs' ambitions to advance in the political system. MPs who are able to read a text in English, French, and/or German have a more distinct connection to interest in prominent positions. Experience that MPs acquired through activity or positions in voluntary organizations and faith communities, however, seems not to contribute to their potential career ambitions. The reverse is instead the case: MPs who have no prior experience with voluntary organizations are more interested in prominent political positions.

Table 4.2 Proportion of potentially ambitious MPs and their socioeconomic resources

	Potential career ambitions (%)	Difference (%)	Number of persons
Occupation when elected			
Small business owner/farmer	0		13
Blue-collar worker	11		18
White-collar worker	12		123
Professional politician	29	29**	87
Prior experience with voluntary organizations			
Yes, hold/have held a position	17		241
No	24	7	38
Language skills			
Worse	10		79
Better	21	11***	16

Source: Parliamentary Study 1996.

Note: The difference was calculated by subtracting the lowest value from the highest value for each of the MPs' resources. The voluntary organizations include professional associations, trade unions, business/industry organizations, women's organizations, environmental organizations, and religious organizations/churches/faith communities. Language skills are based on the MPs' self-assessment of their own language skills. The question was "Can you read a simple text in the following languages?" The list of languages included English, French, and German. The options were "Yes, with no difficulty," "Yes, with some difficulty," and "No." The variables have been merged into an index for this study. The MPs who have an average score indicating that they can at least read a simple text in all three languages are assessed as having greater language skills. The other MPs are assessed as having lesser language skills. *$p < .10$, **$p < .05$, ***$p < .01$.

THE MPS' CAREER AMBITIONS AND ENGAGEMENT

People who are interested in politics have a shorter route to political participation. In the American study, political engagement was divided into four dimensions: political interest, political efficacy, political information, and partisanship (Verba, Schlozman, and Brady 1995:345ff).

That a full-time politician is likely to be interested in politics, identify with a party, have a reasonable general education, and have faith in the political system may seem fairly obvious. But by studying the age at which MPs joined their parties, we can gain an understanding through the 1996 Parliamentary Study of whether there is any connection between early engagement and career ambition.

An American study undertaken in 1966 found evidence that the earlier citizens became interested in politics, the more likely they were to have ambitions for political power (Prewitt, Eulau, and Zisk 1966). Looking at the situation in Sweden, there seems to be a correlation between when politicians joined their parties and how far they have progressed in their careers (at least on the aggregated level). The average age at which local politicians in Sweden joined their parties is thirty-one (Karlsson 2001:149). Members of the parliament joined their parties a few years earlier. If we look at the MPs in 1996, the average age was just under twenty-five. There is thus a difference of six years between parliamentarians and local politicians at the start of their partisan engagement.

Because the results of *Exit Riksdagen* (Ahlbäck Öberg, Hermansson, and Wängnerud 2007) were made available to me, I was afforded the opportunity to study the correlation between political engagement in youth and the age at which MPs joined their parties. *Exit Riksdagen* looked at 114 MPs who sat in the parliament during the 1994–1998 term and did not, for various reasons, stay in office for another term. These individuals were asked about aspects including their interest in politics and social engagement in their youth. Of those who reported that they were fairly interested or very interested in politics as youth, 72 percent had joined their parties before age twenty-six. Among those who were less interested in politics in youth, only 26 percent were members of a political party at that age. The correlation remains even after controlling for socioeconomic factors. MPs who were very interested in politics thus joined a party earlier than did less interested MPs—with the likely conclusion being that individuals who join political parties at a young age are often highly engaged in politics.

If we look at the survey material from 1996, we see that MPs with potential career ambition became involved in partisan politics on average two years earlier than their colleagues and became active in their parties at about age twenty-three whereas their colleagues entered politics when they were past the age of twenty-five. One might also say that a parliamentarian with potential career ambition had already been a party member for eight years at the point the local politician decided to get involved.

If we then study what proportion of MPs joined their parties by age twenty, a certain difference is revealed. More than half the potentially ambitious MPs joined their parties before the age of twenty-one. Of the MPs who claim to have no career ambitions, one-third had joined their parties by the same age. Politicians who do not report having any political career ambition seem to get involved somewhat later in life, although there is no dramatic difference in the average age between the two groups. Because there is a correlation between age and potential career ambitions, it is probably a good idea to exclude MPs over age fifty-five in the analysis. However, even if we just compare MPs under fifty-five with each other, the result remains intact: MPs with potential career ambitions commit themselves to party politics at an earlier age.

MPS' CAREER AMBITIONS AND RECRUITMENT

Recruitment is an important ingredient in political participation. The transition from engagement to participation often happens when a person is asked to get involved in a political activity (Verba, Schlozman, and Brady 1995:157). Studies of politicians' willingness to run for election also have shown that encouragement from political actors is a central component in political engagement (Fox and Lawless 2010; see also Schunk and Lilly 1984). People who are encouraged to participate are four times more likely to be willing to run for political office than people who were not encouraged (Lawless and Fox 2005:100).

Career politicians in Sweden have also emphasized the importance of collegial support (Niklasson 2005). More than half of newly elected representatives at the local level report that they entered politics at the urging of others (Karlsson 2001:146). It is less clear whether this also affects career ambition per se. MPs in the parliament have of course already been recruited, but they may have been recruited for elective office in the party organization to a varying extent. Recruitment to leading positions in the organization may induce an MP to begin considering a bid to climb the career ladder.

The 1996 Parliamentary Study makes it possible to compare various types of board positions in the party organization and the extent to which the MPs hold or have held leading positions on party boards. Whether or not the MPs have experience of holding these positions is used as an indicator of recruitment.

Table 4.3 shows that there are differences between recruitment and which MPs have potential career ambitions. In respect to party board positions at the national and international levels, the tendency is that the potential career politicians have been recruited to a higher extent. The percentage of potentially ambitious MPs who hold or have held a central position in the party is more than twice as high as that of other MPs. This may indicate that members who aspire to move up in the hierarchy have been given more encouragement from the party at the central level and have consequently become more interested in a continued career. It cannot be precluded, however, that potentially ambitious MPs are those who are better at maneuvering themselves into the top echelons of the party, and it is therefore difficult to say anything about the direction of the correlation (more about this in Chapter 6, when we will study possible career attainments). Nevertheless, potentially ambitious MPs have not consistently been favored in recruitment to various board positions within the party organization. But of the five types of board posi-

Table 4.3 Comparison of MPs' recruitment to board positions in the party organization

Have now or previously held a board position in the party?	Potential career ambitions (%)		Difference (%)	Number of persons
	Yes	No		
Party on the international level	11	5	6	15
Party organization on the national level	38	18	20***	55
Auxiliary party organizations on the national level	31	20	11*	57
Party organization on the local/ regional level	80	90	–10*	226
Auxiliary party organizations on the local/regional level	27	29	–2	73

Source: Parliamentary Study 1996.

Note: The balance measure shows the difference between those who hold or have held board positions in the party organization. As MPs may have had more than one position, the results do not add up to 100 percent. $*p < .10, **p < .05, ***p < .01$.

tions listed on Table 4.3, potential career politicians were more prominent in three of the cases.

Recruitment networks may also have to do with where people live and the circles in which they move (Verba, Schlozman, and Brady 1995, chapter 5). The MPs' workplace—the House of Parliament—is in the capital, Stockholm. There is only one center of political power in Sweden, the Stockholm region. Can proximity to Stockholm entail that such a center of power attracts more people with career ambitions? Prior research has shown, for example, that US state legislatures that invest in providing political staff and higher pay also attract younger, more career-oriented individuals (Maestas et al. 2006). In this case, recruitment is not a matter of having been encouraged to move to constituencies in and around Stockholm; the Stockholm area in and of itself constitutes a base of recruitment for those interested in a career in politics.

In Table 4.4 we study the proportion of potentially ambitious MPs in the Stockholm area compared to elsewhere in the country.

Proportionately speaking, there are undeniably more MPs with potential career ambition in constituencies in the Stockholm area than in the rest of Sweden. MPs from the Stockholm area demonstrate higher interest in prominent positions than do MPs whose base is elsewhere. When I study interest in prominent positions in and around the second and the third biggest cities in Sweden—

Table 4.4 Proportion of potential career politicians in the Stockholm area and the rest of the country

	Potential career ambitions (%)	Difference (%)	Number of persons
Stockholm area	39		
Rest of the country	12	27***	281

Source: 1996 Parliamentary Study.
Note: The Stockholm area consists of constituencies in Stockholm, Uppsala, and Södermanland. The difference is calculated by subtracting the percentage of potential career politicians in Stockholm from the percentage of potential career politicians in the rest of the country. $*p < .10$, $**p < .05$, $***p < .01$.

Gothenburg and Malmö—the results are completely different: for the Gothenburg area, the number is 9 percent, and in the Malmö the figure is zero.

A complementary explanation for why potential career politicians reside in or near Stockholm concerns distance. Proximity to the House of Parliament may make it easier to imagine a continued career in politics. One of the factors tested in the previously cited study *Exit Riksdagen* was the effect of distance upon the likelihood of MPs to leave office. The results, however, pointed to the opposite: MPs who lived in the Stockholm area tended to find it easier to leave their positions (2007:55f). We cannot rule out that one reason for leaving was that these individuals had a greater selection of other appealing positions available to them, making the decision to leave the parliament easier. Regardless, the "close to the job" hypothesis seems to have no bearing on who stays in politics and consequently is unlikely to bring us closer to explaining the concentration of potential career politicians in the Stockholm area.

CAREER AMBITION AND PARTY AFFILIATION

Before I test the validity of the various correlations in a regression analysis, I must consider the relationship between political parties and potential career politicians. In the beginning of this chapter I said that there are primarily two patterns of interest. The first, the strategy pattern, aligns with the Social Democrats alone or in combination with the Conservative Party having the highest proportion of potential career politicians. The second pattern is constituted of party cultures; differences between the parties on the role of the individual MP in relation to the party collective. The party culture pattern indicates that in Sweden, the parties that should have potentially ambitious MPs are the Green Party, the Liberal Party, and the Left Party. The percentage of potentially ambitious MPs in each party is shown in Table 4.5.

Table 4.5 Proportion of potentially ambitious MPs by party

Party affiliation	Potential career ambition (%)	Number of persons
Center Party	13	24
Social Democratic Party	13	128
Liberal Party	20	20
Christian Democratic Party	20	20
Conservative Party	21	63
Left Party	22	18
Green Party	46	13

Source: Parliamentary Study 1996.

As the table illustrates, neither the Social Democrats nor the Conservatives have a proportionately higher number of potential career politicians. Nor do the cultural patterns of the Liberal Party, Green Party, and Left Party differ from those of the other parties. Six of the parties are within a range of 9 percentage points. None of the differences between the parties are statistically significant. As different party cultures do exist, the differences between the parties should be somewhat more apparent.

There is, however, one party that is a true outlier, the Green Party. The Greens are much more career-oriented than MPs from the other parties. The result is somewhat surprising in light of the party's bylaws, which impose a limit of three terms or twelve years on their MPs. Despite this, nearly half of the Green MPs indicate aspirations to continue their political careers. In addition, when the survey was undertaken, the Green Party had just made it back to the parliament. After the first term in which it had won seats, 1988–1991, the party lost its seats in parliament in the next election.

The results become less difficult to interpret if we return to Barrling Hermansson's thesis. In her analysis of the Greens' party culture, Barrling Hermansson emphasized that the party sets itself apart by having no distinct party culture (2004:238). Due to inadequate empirical evidence, Barrling Hermansson was conservative in her interpretation of the results, but she argued that her study and others show that the Greens in the parliament want to reduce the influence of the party group and would prefer individual MPs to have more influence and stronger status (ibid., 239).

The differences are small among the other parties with regard to the proportion of potentially ambitious MPs, and so it does not seem that the MPs choose which party to join based on strategic considerations or that large parties awaken political career ambitions in their MPs. Instead, it is the smallest party in the parliament at the time the survey was taken, and the party with the most uncertain political future that has a large proportion of potentially ambitious MPs. One interpretation is that the most goal-oriented Greens chose to make another bid for the Riksdagen. In order to win seats in the parliament, the Green Party gave latitude to candidates who were highly motivated and prepared to act in order to succeed. More hesitant individuals, or individuals who needed a strong party organization, found it more difficult to assert themselves under these conditions.[7] As well, a party that does not have strong collective values also does not rein in or constrain people with potential career ambitions.

WHO ARE THE POTENTIALLY AMBITIOUS MPS?

The data presented in the tables thus far have indicated that there may be systematic differences based on the MPs' socioeconomic status and their aspirations. In this section I will use a multivariate regression analysis to test the factors presented in the foregoing sections. Three models will be studied. The first includes the factors brought forward in research on political participation. These components will be augmented in the second model with the more precisely defined components presented by Verba, Schlozman, and Brady. The third model will include the political parties.

Table 4.6 shows that the explanatory model used to identify which MPs may have career ambitions is a good start. Model 1 shows that the MPs' family background is significant. MPs who come from blue-collar homes are less likely to have potential career ambitions. Also noteworthy is that the correlation is strengthened when controlled for factors related to resources, commitment, and recruitment. Upon more detailed testing, it emerges that family background is particularly important for women with potential career ambitions. Women who grew up in a blue-collar home are less likely to have potential career ambitions than men in the same position. Age also has an effect. Older MPs are less likely than younger MPs to be potential career politicians. The significance of age also reinforces the impression that the MPs have understood that the positions are in the future and that older MPs choose to refrain for that reason.

When we expand on model 1 with model 2, it becomes clear that the MPs who were professional politicians when they were elected to the parliament are among the occupational group in which potential career politicians are found. Professional politicians live for and in politics to a greater extent than others. That MPs with this background are not only aiming for career attainment in general but aspire to the highest positions becomes especially clear if the definition of career ambition is augmented with positions such as committee chair and party group leader. As soon as the definition is expanded, the significant correlation between professional politicians and prominent positions is eliminated. Professional politicians thus

Table 4.6 Relationship of background factors to potential career ambition (logistic regression, odds ratio)

	Model 1	Model 2	Model 3
Socioeconomic status			
Female	.803	1.251	1.115
Family background	2.566*	4.873**	5.965*
Education	2.019	1.245	1.058
Age	1.071***	1.063**	1.063**
Resources			
Professional politicians		3.111**	4.082**
Voluntary organization		1.070	.436
Language skills		4.112**	5.293**
Commitment			
Joined the party		.983	.950*
Recruitment			
Party, central		1.172	1.211
Capital area		3.234**	3.341**
Political party			
Center Party			2.671
Christian Democratic Party			1.833
Conservative Party			1.105
Green Party			17.017**
Left Party			6.984*
Liberal Party			1.860
Pseudo R^2	.113***	.250***	.310***
Number of persons	214	190	190

Sources: Parliamentary Study 1994, 1996.
Note: Dependent variable: 0 = No career ambition, 1 = Career ambition. Independent variables: Family background: 0 = Father blue collar, 1 = Father white-collar/small business owner; Education: 0 = Not university educated, 1 = University educated; Age: Serial by year of birth; Voluntary organization: 0 = No experience of board positions, 1 = Experience. Language skills are based on the MPs self-reported language skills. MPs who have an average score indicating that they can read a simple text in three languages are assessed as having superior language skills = 1. The other MPs are assessed as having lesser language skills = 0. Joined the party: Serial 10–52 years; MPs who have board positions within the central party organization = 1, Those who have not held or no longer had board positions = 0; Capital area: 0 = Electoral districts outside the Stockholm area, 1 = Municipality of Stockholm, Stockholm County, Södermanland County, and Uppsala County. The Social Democratic Party is the reference category. *p < .10, **p < .05, ***p < .01. Robust standard errors.

differ from the others in their distinct ambitions to achieve the most prominent positions outside the parliament.

Among the other factors in the "resources" category, language skills are significant. For politicians who want to be on the main stage, language skills could be helpful when they represent their country on different occasions. Prior experience in civil society does not have a significant correlation to potential career ambition. Commitment to party politics seems to be of some importance. There are, however, good reasons to be cautious. In Model 2 and Model 3 the commitment for party politics is not under control for age. The reason for this is that a young MP can hardly have been involved in politics when he or she was somewhat older. When both age and party commitment are included in the regression model, neither are significant. Age and commitment to party politics is therefore correlated. It is also difficult to establish whether youth as such encourages ambition, or if it is the commitment that attracts some MPs to politics at an early age. For these reasons I think it is wise to be cautious.

A certain type of recruitment also seems related to potential career ambition. MPs based in the Stockholm area are more likely to report that they are interested in a continued political career. However, encouragement in the form of leading positions within the party organization does not seem to have significant effect. Nor do the results shown on the table provide any support for the notion that Social Democratic MPs are more ambitious than others, or that large parties attract potentially ambitious MPs. Instead, MPs of the Green Party and, to a lesser extent, the Left Party appear to be the most ambitious. When the party affiliation is redefined as a two-tailed variable and run for each party separately, the Left Party does not deviate from the other parties while the Green Party does.

WHO HAS POTENTIAL CAREER AMBITIONS?

The results presented in this chapter confirm that the definition of career ambition we have applied can be related to factors that are well understood within the research on political participation. If we attempt to predict which background factors will distinguish an MP with potential career ambitions, we arrive at the following picture: a person who is thirty years old, a professional politician when elected, a resident of the capital area, with language skills, and whose family background is not blue collar has an estimated probability of 86 percent of harboring potential career ambitions.[8] If the MP is also a member of the Green Party, the figure rises to 99 percent. At the other end of the scale, a person who is sixty years old, from a blue-collar family, based outside the capital area, and was not a professional politician when elected to the parliament has not even a predicted probability of

1 percent of harboring potential career ambitions. This is crucial to the validation of the survey question. Based on the survey question about future top-level positions, there is a classification that relates to prior experiences in the MPs' lives. Potential career politicians are not randomly distributed in the parliament. Certain determinants facilitate the prediction of which MPs have the highest probability of possessing potential career ambitions. This indicates that the MPs who reported an interest in prominent positions meant something when they "confessed" their future plans.

One important aspect remains, however, before we can talk about ambitious MPs. According to the adopted definition, the MPs must not only be committed, working over the long-term, and goal-oriented; in order to establish that the MPs have career ambitions, we also need to connect the thus far only potential career politicians with specific behavior. We must be able to preclude that the potential career politicians are not merely expressing a desire. One interpretation of the results that have thus far emerged is that potential career politicians primarily *aspire* to attain influential positions. What we do not know is whether they are taking action to achieve their lofty goals. This means that the picture of potential career politicians thus far in the story might very well accurately describe politicians who are simply plodding along and waiting to see what happens. With hard work, they hope to one day be given the opportunity, but they are not taking any particular action to improve their chances. In order to determine whether this group really consists of ambitious MPs, the next chapter will be devoted to the question of what potential career politicians do at party group meetings and in the plenary assembly, and how they orient themselves in the role of representative.

5. Are There MPs with Real Career Ambitions?

We have been able to determine that there are MPs who have expressed an interest in more prominent positions and that they are a distinguishable group among parliamentarians. This group has what I call *potential career ambition*. For MPs with potential career ambition to qualify as MPs with "real" career ambitions, additional requirements must be met. According to the definition discussed in Chapter 2, it should be possible to link certain behavior to MPs career ambitions. The purpose of this chapter is therefore to put the spotlight on the MPs' behavior. Accordingly, in the following section ambition is tested as an explanatory factor in what occurs in and around the parliament.

AMBITION AND BEHAVIOR

The definition of *career ambition* does not specify what kind of actions an MP must take for the behavior to be linked to ambition to make a career in politics. I will compare two scenarios, the first involving ambitious MPs whose strategy is to adjust to party norms in order to curry favor with party leadership, and the second involving ambitious MPs who engage in more outward-directed action in order to cultivate a distinct reputation that makes them attractive within the party. I will soon develop my argument, but first something about the state of research.

Research on how ambitious MPs behave in party-centric environments is sparse. Swedish researchers have found that once MPs are no longer seeking re-election, they lose interest in their home constituencies (Esaiasson and Holmberg 1996). Lars Davidsson (2006) showed in his thesis that "vulnerable" MPs—that is, MPs at risk of losing their seats—work harder to promote regional issues.

These results are interesting because they suggest that MPs assign value to their constituencies differently depending on whether they want to remain in the parliament. However, this says little about what is important to MPs who are seeking a long-term career.

Research from the United States shows that politicians who want to advance from the state level to the national scene pursue broader issues to attract more voters. The American research also shows that national representatives who want to continue their political careers adapt their behavior in Congress in order to put themselves in the "right" position in relation to their base (Francis and Kenny 1996, 2000; Hibbing 1986; Treul 2009; Van Der Slik and Pernacciaro 1979). A strong position in the home district is a fundamental prerequisite for American politicians who aspire to career attainment (Box-Steffensmeier et al. 2003; Cain, Ferejohn, and Fiorina 1987; Feldman and Jondrow, 1984; McAdams and Johannes 1987; Parker and Parker 1985). The American research has, however, been disputed. Rebekah Herrick, whose criticism was presented in Chapter 2, has argued that American scholars cannot actually say anything about members' ambitions because the members themselves have not been asked about their future plans. Instead, the researchers' analyses are based on studies of the members' behavior, with focus on their willingness to run for office. According to Herrick, much of what scholars claim about the behavior of American members, and which has been linked to ambition, may have been overestimated because the measure of ambition is flawed (Herrick 2001).

Overall, one can say that research into the behavior of ambitious politicians in party-centric settings is thin and that American research on political ambition has problems with the operational indicator. In light of these two factors, I will proceed to look at the two aforementioned scenarios.

Scenario One: Lie Low

In the first scenario, ambitious MPs are people who make an effort to fit in and not stand out. There are recurring descriptions of how MPs picked up by the party leadership have been "spineless" and refrained from voicing their opinion when the party leadership so demanded. One such description can be read in Per Gahrton's 1983 thesis, *Inside the Riksdag: A Study of Parliamentary Paralysis in Response to a Society in Crisis*. Gahrton made a much-discussed attempt to use his notes to systematize impressions of life inside the party during his own tenure in the parliament.[1] He argued that total alignment with prevailing party norms was the royal road for those seeking status (1983:68). Gahrton's work has been criticized for being too speculative (see, e.g., Hagevi 1995). In my search for how the MPs themselves describe the situation in the parliament, however, I have seen recurring instances of disgruntled MPs who maintain that party loyalty overshadows almost everything else: "Loyalty to the party leadership is set above all. For the major parties, all they have to do is find people who are not color blind and can tell the difference between the red and green voting buttons in the parliament" (MP Ann-Marie Pålsson explaining in an interview why she was not running for election to parliament in 2010).[2]

The colorful Liberal MP Birgitta Ohlsson described the prerequisites, at least before she became a cabinet minister, for a successful career as follows: "The tall poppy syndrome lies over this house of parliament like a wet blanket. [...] Loyalty is still rewarded above all, not opposing the leadership, not rocking the boat. The best strategy for a young politician to succeed today—and I say this with a heavy heart—is to be ambitious, but not too ambitious, be highly malleable, and stay in the good graces of party leadership. If they do, the career ladder will go straight up" (*Dagens Nyheter*, 15 September 2008). Another example comes from MP Sven Bergström. When asked whether there is any obvious answer to how an MP should behave when voting in the parliament, he responded, "No, it depends on things like the nature of the issue and the MP's convictions. But also on your career ambitions. If you are ambitious, you should be very careful about voting against your own party and your party leadership. If you do, you burn your bridges" (ibid.). Former Center Party MP Solveig Ternström also associated a political career with adaptability and argued that senior citizens in politics could make a difference because they have the courage to stand up for their convictions: "We seniors [have] an advantage that is rarely mentioned. We have the courage to be honest and straightforward because to us it is not the end of the world if we do not make it onto the ballot list in four years. We are not thinking about our careers, we are thinking about policy" (*Expressen*, 6 October 2009).

In an interview with former MPs, the benefit of being able to hold one's tongue is also shown: "You have to have *fingerspitzgefühl* [in essence, tact]. A sense of when you can stand out and when you cannot. You should not talk too much at party group meetings. I have learned that by watching others' mistakes" (Isberg 1999:67).[3] When long-time parliamentarian Per Edvin Sköld, who sat in the parliament from 1918 to 1964, shared his experiences with a first-term MP, his advice was, "Wait to request the floor until you have something significant to say. If one day you should happen to feel you have a really good rebuttal—save it. There are sure to be occasions when it will be even more apt" (Larsson 1996:232).

Based on these statements, one might believe that MPs aspiring to influential positions should be amenable and align themselves utterly with party norms. However, I cannot disabuse myself of the notion that the MPs' statements are indicative of the critical attitude toward political ambition and that MPs who are discontented with life in parliament judge their colleagues in a less flattering light.

Scenario Two: Cultivate a Personal Reputation

In the second scenario, ambitious MPs are people who believe in themselves and crave attention. I have taken inspiration from *US Senators and Their World* (Matthews 1960). In this book, Donald Matthews laid out the details of life in the US Senate. Addressing the issue of the senators' ambitions, Matthews contended that senators who want to advance are forced to make themselves stand out. He concluded, "As a general rule, it seems that a man who entirely adheres to the Senate folkways has little chance of becoming President of the United States" (Matthews 1959: 1080).[4] According to Matthews, a politician who wants to reach the heights cannot rely on following the "rule book" but must sometimes break with convention. To become known, a politician must quite simply have the courage to be provocative. Taking this scenario to a more general level, Bernard Manin (1996) has argued that all of representative democracy is moving toward an audience democracy, in which the candidates' personal traits will take on increasing importance.

As persona becomes more pivotal, it also becomes more important for politicians to be seen and bring attention to themselves. As a result, Manin believed that the old political elite would be replaced: "What we are witnessing today is not a departure from the principles of representative, but a change in the types of elites that are selected. Elections continue to elevate to office individuals who possess distinctive features; they retain the elitist character they always had. However, a new elite of experts in communication has replaced the political activist and the party bureaucrat. Audience democracy is the rule of the *media expert*" (1996:220). In such a case, this would indicate that the parties would have to take a step back in favor of a new breed of politician and that the importance of self-marketing will be a factor to reckon with.[5]

Regardless of what the future brings, the upshot of scenario two is that ambitious MPs must persuade their own organization. Excessive loyalty to the party leadership seems not to be appreciated by colleagues in the parliament (if we can believe the quotations presented in the beginning of the chapter). One way of handling collegial mistrust of people who obey the party leadership in word and deed may be to vote against the party line on suitable occasions, or to be responsive to party opinion and draw attention to a modicum of independence. If this is true, a politician aiming for a long-term career needs to cultivate a personal reputation.[6]

From these two scenarios I have derived a number of hypotheses that will help me look for patterns in the MPs' behavior. I have chosen two relatively obvious points of departure as the basis for my search: the MPs' attitudes toward aspects that relate to their role as elected representatives, and their more specific attitudes toward their party organization. More specifically, I base my examination on questions in the Parliamentary Studies where MPs were given an opportunity to explain their views on the actual office of representative and how they organize their work as a member of parliament. We can thus see two types of strategic organization. In the first scenario, the party and party cohesion are what matter. Ambitious MPs do not want to trigger unnecessary attention; they put the party first and keep a low profile in the hope that their loyalty will be rewarded. In the second scenario, the individual takes on a more central role. These MPs attempt by various means to make an impression in order to gain attention and be considered for recruitment to various positions.

There are, however, circumstances that suggest that both scenarios are wrong. In this chapter as well, I am wrestling with problems related to the study of political ambition. Swedish parliamentary studies have certainly found evidence that there is some scope for internal factors as explanations for MPs' behavior (Davidsson 2006; Esaiasson and Holmberg 1996; Hagevi 1998). The main rule, though, is that the parties assume the role of central agents. Research has also focused on what can best explain members' career attainment (although without taking personal ambition into account). The research has concluded that reelection is the most important factor in carving out a successful political career in the Swedish parliament (Hagevi 1998). MPs who have sat in the parliament for a long time have the greatest opportunities for career attainment. This rotation rule may have implications for our search for distinguishable behavior. The seniority principle may influence MPs against deciding to behave in a specific manner.

If the seniority principle is the key, the main objective is having the perseverance to remain in the parliament; in such a situation, it is by no means expected that the MPs will take any particular action other than just hanging on in the parliament. It has also emerged in preceding chapters that politicians who "reveal" their career ambitions may face collegial opposition. MPs who are categorized as career-oriented by others are also considered less fitting candidates.

It is also possible that MPs seeking influential positions engage in strategic behavior, but that this is not evident in the material. There is thus risk that I will be "fooled" by the absence of an action-oriented pattern. If no differences between the MPs can be found, we will have a choice to make. Either I have found MPs who have no career ambition in any real sense, or the available survey material does not provide the aspects that best pick up ambitious politicians' patterns of movement.

One way of bringing clarity to the issue is offered in the next chapter. In Chapter 6, I will study the MPs' actual careers between 1996 and 2006. If I find that potentially ambitious MPs do either better or worse than others, it may be an indicator that MPs have behaved in a manner that had consequences for their careers. Likewise, a result showing that the careers of MPs with aspirations for advancement have not developed any better or any worse than those of other MPs may be accepted as evidence that while they had some hopes for advancement, they made no active attempt to improve their careers. This remains to be seen, however, and we will first compare the two scenarios. The search for distinguishable behavior begins with how the MPs view their jobs as elected representatives and how they prioritize their work in the parliament. Thereafter, the search will focus on whether potentially ambitious MPs engage in specific behavior vis-à-vis party-internal conditions. This has to do with how MPs orient themselves internally within the

party and the strategic choices they make. We begin by studying whether there is any correlation between the MPs' aspirations and how they view their jobs as elected representatives.

AMBITION AND REPRESENTATION

In the first test, the relationship between how the MPs view the role of elected representative and their possible career ambitions will be incorporated into a classic context. There has been a traditional difference of opinion on how representation should be practiced. The dividing line has gone between those inspired by the idea that MPs should follow the instructions of their constituencies and those who believe that representatives should primarily follow their personal convictions (Eulau et al. 1959).[7] In the first version, the politician is a *delegate*; in the second version he or she is a free agent, or *trustee*. Delegates should conform to voters' opinions whereas trustees are required to use their reasoned judgment to determine what is best for the country and its population.

The most famous advocate of the "representative governed by reason" is Edmund Burke (Pitkin 1967). Burke's ideas celebrated trustees' greatest triumphs before the advent of the strong party system. In the early 1900s, the parties took over, giving rise to a different approach to the principles of representation. The bound and unbound mandates were augmented with the party mandate. The party mandate, as the name suggests, says that representatives primarily represent their party.

The party mandate has been widely accepted in Sweden, and an overwhelming majority of MPs in the Riksdagen consider themselves party delegates first and foremost (see, e.g., Esaiasson and Holmberg 1996; Holmberg 1974; for an overview of the literature on representation see Rehfeld 2009). In the 1996 Parliamentary Study, MPs were asked to state how important a number of tasks were to them personally, including representing their party, themselves, and their voters. Is there a relationship between what the MPs prioritize in the role of elected representative based on their seeking of influential positions? Table 5.1 shows that there is.

MPs who had indicated interest in influential positions distinguish themselves as soon as it comes to the more fundamental questions having to do with representation. We can see that these MPs differ significantly in three out of four representation styles. Table 5.1 indicates that the home constituency is less important to potentially ambitious MPs. The predicted probability for a MP with potential career ambition to consider it to be very important to represent their own constituency is 24 percent. That is more than a 50 percentage-point decrease compared to MPs who do not strive upward. They have a predicted probability of 40 percent to see the constituency as very important. This might be considered surprising from

Table 5.1 MPs' estimations of which principles of representation are very
important to them personally (ordinal-logistic regression, odds ratio)

	Represent the constituency	Represent individual voters	Represent the party platform	Represent my own convictions
Career ambition	.433*	.261**	1.199	2.031*
Female	1.559	1.030	2.552**	1.260
Family background	.872	.863	1.232	.878
Education	.936	1.431	.664	1.344
Age	.966	.994	3.116**	1.014
Professional politician	.878	1.268	.948**	.749
Seniority	.954*	1.015	.997	1.031
Status	.637	.680	.798	.527
Political party				
Center Party	.839	1.552	.363	2.080
Christian Democratic Party	.364	1.420	4.543	3.366*
Conservative Party	.277**	1.205	.436*	2.466**
Green Party	.028***	2.040	1.319	1.379
Left Party	.204**	2.336	.938	1.452
Liberal Party	.208**	1.575	1.020	9.725**
Pseudo R^2	.144	.047	.085	.068
Number of persons	201	200	200	200

Source: Parliamentary Study 1996.
Note: The survey question was, "How important are the following tasks for you personally
as a member of parliament?" The alternatives included, "My party's platform," "Important
convictions (personally)," "My region/constituency's interests/convictions," and "The
problems of individual voters/people." The options were 1 = Not important at all, 2 = Fairly
unimportant, 3 = Fairly important, and 4 = Very important. The independent variables are
coded as follows: Career ambition: 0 = No career ambition, 1 = Career ambition; Female:
0 = Male, 1 = Female; Family background: 0 = Father blue-collar, 1 = Father small business
owner or white-collar; Education: 0 = Not university educated, 1 = University educated;
Occupation: 0 = Blue-collar, small business owner, and white-collar, 1= Professional
politician; Age: Serially according to age; Seniority: Serially by number of years in the
parliament; Status: 0 = Have never held or have held a central party position, 1 = Have now
a central party position. The Social Democratic Party is the reference category. *p <.1, **p <
.05, ***p < .001. Robust standard errors.

an American perspective. We have already discussed the importance of electoral
districts in the American system.

In his groundbreaking work on how American congressional representatives
interact with constituents "at home," Richard Fenno was able to describe how critical the home district is to the politician's personal career. According to Fenno
(1978), members of Congress work hard to "fit in" in their districts and must de-

vote time, resources, and commitment in order to do so. Home constituencies are not, however, of the same importance to Swedish potentially ambitious MPs, but rather the reverse.[8]

If one augments the results shown on Table 5.1 with that shown by Davidsson (2006), the MPs who are "fighting" to remain in the parliament are those who devote time and resources to their home constituencies, and those who have higher ambitions have their sights aimed in a different direction.[9] Likewise, Kaare Strøm assumed that MPs who are aiming for the top must be ready to please the upper echelon of the party: "A successful aspirant to party office must therefore be willing to devote time and energy to party objectives, even if that means neglecting one's local constituency" (1997:169). Maybe that is a part of the reason why ambitious MPs do not focus on their constituencies. In another study, Cain, Ferejohn, and Fiorina (1987) compared the importance of constituency service in Great Britain and the United States. They found that members in both legislative bodies devote much of their time to help people in their constituencies. Moreover, they found that in the Westminster system, constituency service matters for electoral success. The authors also discussed proportional electoral systems, including those in the Scandinavian countries. They concluded that there are circumstances indicating that constituency service is of smaller importance in Scandinavia than elsewhere, and these are: the assemblies have to a lesser extent been professionalized, the willingness to actually be reelected is rather low, the idea of ombudsman is a formal institution, and the parliaments are centralized and the party leaders are in control of the internal party organization (1987:223ff). It makes less sense to build a strong base among voters when ultimately it is the party elite who will decide your political future.

With this in mind, it comes as no surprise that the convictions of individual voters are not of any significant interest to potentially ambitious MPs. If we look at the percentage distribution between potentially ambitious MPs and their colleagues concerning the importance of interacting with individual voters, large differences emerge. Only 14 percent of potentially ambitious MPs consider it very important to represent individual voters whereas 33 percent of other MPs think this is a very important task. In other words, the constituency and individual voters are deprioritized areas for potentially ambitious MPs. The importance of representing the party platform, however, does not distinguish potentially ambitious MPs. Instead, those who most clearly prioritize the party platform are women and professional politicians.

According to the results shown on Table 5.1, potentially ambitious MPs value the importance of representing their own convictions, which relates to the scenario that says that MPs with career ambitions base their actions on themselves and cultivate a personal reputation. Potentially ambitious MPs have a predicted probability of 59 percentage points to stress the importance of their own convictions while their colleagues have a probability of 42 percentage points.[10]

It is noteworthy that this result agrees with an older American study from the 1960s. In that study, John Soule (1969) found that Edmund Burke's classical conception of the worthy legislator was most closely reflected by legislators at the state level (Michigan) who held progressive ambitions. They had a high propensity to use their own judgment, were less interested in their own districts, and oriented their concern toward the state as a whole. Soule's results were not based on a sophisticated analysis but may be an indicator of a commonality between Burke's principles and political ambition.

Potentially ambitious MPs consider it important to represent their own convictions and are less interested in their own constituencies and individual voters. In Burke's conception, there is a conflict between what the voters think and what is actually best for the country. The representative must therefore be able to separate the voters' opinions from their true interests.[11] For this reason, it may be interesting to stay with Burke's ideas on worthy representation for a moment. In his famous speech of 1774, Burke remarked, "Parliament is a deliberative assembly of one nation, with one interest, that of the whole; where, not local purposes, not local prejudices, ought to guide, but the general good, resulting from the general reason of the whole. You choose a member indeed; but when you have chosen him, he is not member of Bristol, but he is a member of parliament."[12]

A member of parliament should, according to Burke, put the interests of the nation first and not devote much time to catering to special interests. The questions in the 1996 Parliamentary Study included one that deals with the parliament as an institution and which elements of their parliamentary work the MPs consider important. The alternatives included two aspects with a connection to Edmund Burke and his representative ideal ("articulate public needs and interests" and "balance conflicting interests in the country"). If both alternatives are combined into a "Burkean index," we see that the potential career politicians also support these Burkean principles. The results are shown in Table 5.2.

Potentially ambitious MPs consider an important element of their work to be representing wide swathes of the public and formulating policy that is broadly accepted. The broader approach to representation aligns well with the ambitions of potential career politicians to one day also represent Sweden.[13] But the agreement with Burke's ideals is not exclusive to potentially ambitious MPs—there is also a gender aspect. To a greater extent than men, women emphasize the importance of representing the interests of the entire country, as do professional politicians and older MPs.

It emerged earlier when potentially ambitious MPs and their relationships to their constituencies were discussed that they, unlike their colleagues, were more

Table 5.2 MPs report their agreement with Burke's principles of representation (OLS regression, standardized beta coefficients)

	Agreement with Burke's principles
Career ambition	.797**
Female	.855**
Family background	−.082
Education	.342
Age	−.307**
Professional politician	.511**
Seniority	−.001
Status	−.056
Political party	
Center Party	−.224
Christian Democratic Party	−.426
Conservative Party	−.849**
Green Party	.209
Left Party	.415
Liberal Party	−.433
R^2	.173
Number of persons	199

Source: Parliamentary Study 1996.
Note: The survey question was, "If you think about your work as an MP, how important are the following elements of your work?" The options that constituted the dependent variable were, "Articulate public needs and interests" and "Balance conflicting interests in the country." The scale went from 1 = "Not important" to 7 = "Very important." The scale is from 0 to 1 in the regression table. The independent variables are coded as follows: Career ambition: 0 = No career ambition, 1 = Career ambition; Female: 0 = Male, 1 = Female; Family background: 0 = Father blue-collar, 1 = Father small business owner or white-collar; Education: 0 = Not university educated, 1 = University educated; Occupation: 0 = Blue-collar, small business owner, and white-collar, 1 = Professional politician; Age: Serially according to age; Seniority: Serially by number of years in the parliament; Status: 0 = Have never held or have held a central party position, 1 = Have now a central party position. The Social Democratic Party is the reference category. *$p < .1$, **$p < .05$, ***$p < .001$. Alpha .51. Robust standard errors.

interested in geographical units beyond their home constituencies. This may be an indicator that potential career politicians are more internationally oriented and have greater interest in the international arena. There is support for such an interpretation to be found in the survey material from 1996, in which the MPs' general interest in international issues was addressed. Table 5.3 shows that potentially ambitious MPs are generally more interested in international policy issues.

As we view the data, a picture of these MPs begins to take shape. To them, the role of representative seems to closely align with an emphasis on themselves per-

Table 5.3 MPs' interest in international issues (ordinal-logistic regression, odds ratio)

	Interest in international issues in general
Career ambition	2.803**
Female	.795
Family background	.652
Education	3.282***
Age	.996
Professional politician	.877
Seniority	1.064**
Status	1.970
Political party	
Center Party	.777
Christian Democratic Party	.618
Conservative Party	1.246
Green Party	1.552
Left Party	.501
Liberal Party	1.253
R^2	.096
Number of persons	198

Source: Parliamentary Study 1996.

Note: The survey question was, "How interested are you in the following policy areas with regard to international issues?" The MPs were presented with 10 policy areas to take a stance on. The response options ranged from 1 = Very interested, 2 = Fairly interested, 3 = Not particularly interested, to 4 = Not interested at all. In the regression model the dependent variable is reversed. The dependent variable is constituted by the option "International issues in general." The independent variables are coded as follows: Career ambition: 0 = No career ambition, 1 = Career ambition; Female: 0 = Male, 1 = Female; Family background: 0 = Father blue-collar, 1 = Father small business owner or white-collar; Education: 0 = Not university educated, 1 = University educated; Occupation: 0 = Blue-collar, small business owner, and white-collar, 1 = Professional politician; Age: Serially according to the year of birth; Seniority: Serially by number of years in the parliament; Status: 0 = Have never held or have held a central party position, 1 = Have now a central party position. The Social Democratic Party is the reference category. *$p < .1$, **$p < .05$, ***$p < .001$. Robust standard errors.

sonally, accompanied by less interest in their constituencies and individual voters. One interpretation of the prioritizations of potentially ambitious MPs is that they set themselves apart from the "little people" and instead feel a sense of affinity with the larger contexts in which the focus is on the nation as a whole and international politics. The ability to communicate and to integrate broader issues is an important part of this.

It may also be that potentially ambitious MPs are not only more interested in international policy issues but also feel a stronger fundamental engagement with the international constituency. When asked with which geographical unit the MPs primarily identified, 20 percent of potential career politicians say "the world." For other MPs it is much lower, only 5 percent. When Richard Fenno shared his experiences from following US senators on the campaign trail, he asked readers to think about election campaigns as something more than related to just election results. "A focus on the campaigning candidate may encourage us to think of campaigns in the context of the candidate's career and constituency connections" (1996:336).

In fact, Fenno seems to have been right. Even if potentially ambitious MPs have declared that they are not particularly interested in representing their constituency, something happens when it is time for election. During the election seasons, they seem to work fairly hard in their constituencies. When asked about their involvement during the 1994 election campaign, it emerges that they were covered by local media more often and ran more intensive election campaigns (in the form of street meetings, door-to-door canvassing, speeches, etc.). The results are significant in a multivariate regression analysis. Hence, the relationship between the constituency and the potentially ambitious MP appears to vary during the term in office. Interest in the constituency rises during campaigns and becomes relatively tangible but is less important in the periods between elections.

This result correlates with Fenno's observation. Also in a party-centered system with low incentives to cultivate a personal relationship with the voters, ambitious politicians see reason to increase their contacts with constituents during campaigns. However, the reason for why Swedish MPs are more active is less clear-cut than it is with members of the US Congress. The mechanism might not be that ambitious MPs do this to strengthen their relationships with the voters but that they work hard to make an impression on the party leadership.

Even so, there is some indication that MPs who have noted interest in influential positions also have a different orientation to their role as elected representative. We will now investigate whether there is a pattern to how potentially ambitious MPs relate to more party-internal conditions.

AMBITION AND STRATEGIC BEHAVIOR

There is, as I mentioned earlier, little systematic evidence for how an MP should behave in relation to the party in order to achieve influential positions. Based on the two scenarios previously outlined, we can conceive of two possible outcomes. In the first, potentially ambitious MPs toe the party line just like everyone else, but they feel more enthusiasm for this principle than their colleagues. In the second, potentially ambitious MPs feel less enthusiasm about the party line because it constrains them from expressing their opinions and thus cultivating their personal reputation. The point is that regardless of which strategy they choose, they must *distinguish themselves* for me to be able to designate them ambitious politicians.

In order to gain clarity in these matters, this section will begin with the question of how the MPs generally view party norms. Thereafter, we will study how they usually behave at party group meetings and in connection with voting in the parliament. We will also study whether the MPs believe there are certain strategies in the chase after influence that are more successful than others and the extent to which they take the party leadership into consideration when they make decisions.

MPS' ATTITUDES TOWARD PARTY NORMS

The 1994 Parliamentary Study provides an opportunity to test the relationship between the MPs and party discipline in two stages. The survey contains questions that have to do with the MPs' attitudes toward prevailing party norms as well as questions about the extent to which they report compliance with the same. The overall picture is that MPs are relatively content with the status quo: about 80 percent of the MPs think "the party norms are fine as they are." However, the MPs who have denoted interest in influential positions are more inclined to want to tighten the rules. The response options "should be higher" and "somewhat higher" have been merged on Table 5.4 with regard to the question about MPs' attitudes toward party norms.

Table 5.4 indicates that potential career politicians at least do not want to tighten the rules within the party group. The difference of 9 percentage points is statistically significant.

Table 5.4 MPs' attitudes toward party norms

Potential career ambition	Demands for party cohesion and party discipline should be higher/somewhat higher
Yes	5%
No	14%
Difference	–9%*
Number of persons	249

Sources: Parliamentary Study 1994, 1996.
Note: The survey question was, "Generally speaking, what do you think of the demands for party cohesion and party discipline in your party?" The response options were, "Should be much higher," "Should be somewhat higher," "Fine as they are," "Should be somewhat lower," and "Should be much lower." $*p < .1$, $**p < .05$, $***p < .001$.

Table 5.5 Proportion of MPs who would like to strengthen party discipline

Potential career ambition	Internal discussions (%)	Follow the party line (%)	Political initiative (%)
Yes	23	0	9
No	38	5	6
Difference	−15**	−5	3
Number of persons	251	251	251

Sources: Parliamentary Study 1994, 1996.

Note: The survey question was, "What do you think about demands for party cohesion and party discipline in your party with regard to compliance with norms for your work in parliament?" The response options were, "Should be much higher than they are now," "Should be somewhat higher than they are now," "Fine as they are now," "Should be somewhat lower than they are now," and "Should be much lower than they are now." The options "Should be much higher" and "Should be somewhat higher" have been combined in the table. $*p < .1$, $**p < .05$, $***p < .001$.

In the 1994 Parliamentary Study, the MPs had the opportunity to more specifically express their thoughts about party norms in the day-to-day work of politics. The percentages of MPs who would like to strengthen party norms to varying degrees are shown on Table 5.5.

Potentially ambitious MPs generally do not seem more inclined to strengthen the party norms. Once again, we can see that potentially ambitious MPs want to express their own opinions. A markedly lower proportion of potentially ambitious MPs wants to limit opportunities to conduct internal discussions. A somewhat higher proportion would like to see stronger norms related to political initiative, but the difference is not significant. The main impression is thus that potentially ambitious MPs are not in any case endeavoring to bring about a tightening of party norms.[14]

In that respect, the differences that have come to light do not support the first scenario, although none of the reported differences is significant in multivariate regression models. Nonetheless, we can determine that there is some variation between the potential career politicians and the others with respect to their normative attitudes toward issues related to party discipline. Whether this has any consequences for how the MPs later report their behavior remains to be seen.

MPS' BEHAVIOR AT PARTY GROUP MEETINGS

As was noted earlier, long-term parliamentarians have cautioned that individual MPs should limit the amount of talking they do at party group meetings. The 1996

Table 5.6 Proportion of MPs who speak at party group meetings

Potential career ambition	Almost every time/usually (%)
Yes	65
No	36
Difference	29***
Number of persons	277

Source: Parliamentary Study 1996.
Note: The survey question was, "Roughly how usual is it for you to express yourself during parliamentary group meetings?" *$p < .1$, **$p < .05$, ***$p < .001$.

Parliamentary Study asked members how often they speak at party group meetings. Table 5.6 reports the percentages of MPs who speak at party group meetings "almost every time" or "usually."

Although the unspoken rule is that MPs should be chary with their contributions during group meetings, the potential career politicians studied here seem not to have been overly influenced by this. On the contrary, an overwhelming majority (65 percent) of potentially ambitious MPs claim that they speak out more often than other MPs. The difference is significant and remains so in a multivariate ordinal logistic regression.[15]

Potential career politicians report to a greater extent than their colleagues that they would like to have less strict rules concerning "internal discussions" and that they believe it is important, as elected representatives, to communicate their own positions. These attitudes align with their behavior of speaking more frequently at party group meetings. Bringing their own opinions to the fore seems to be much more important to potentially ambitious MPs.

THE MPS AND VOTES IN THE PLENARY ASSEMBLY

In this section, focus is on the MPs' behavior in connection with votes in the plenary assembly. Voting in the parliament could be regarded as an MP's most important task. It is in the actual voting procedure that the MP participates to determine whether a bill will be passed or rejected. In most cases the votes are relatively routine, but there are times when the parliamentary situation is uncertain and where an individual MP's decision may play a crucial role. The most famous example is probably Liberal MP Ture Königson, whose abstention in 1959 made it possible for the Social Democratic government to implement its national pension reform. A more contemporary example is when the "FRA" act on military signals intelligence was to be voted on in 2008. A number of center-right MPs were hesitant about their own government's bill, which had to do with military capacity to engage in covert signal surveillance. The government, which had committed to the bill, was facing serious embarrassment. Over a couple of frenetic days, the center-right MPs who did not support the bill were subjected to intense pressure from their party leadership and some were ultimately compelled to give in (Federley 2010). Again, this is an exception; votes in parliament usually proceed with no drama. Swedish party cohesion, in terms of loyalty to the party line in parliamentary votes, is high by international comparison (Jensen 2000).

Earlier I noted that there were MPs in the study who thought the pressure to vote according to the party line was too intense. In these MPs' opinion, support for the party line was something that inhibited them from stating their own opinions. It should, however, be emphasized that MPs who comply with the party line are not necessarily lacking in the courage of their convictions. Party discipline is an important resource, and when party cohesion is upheld, an MP who manages to drive through an issue internally can later count on the support of party colleagues when the issue is voted on in the plenary assembly. Cohesion and discipline also lend the party credibility as a collective actor in negotiations with other parties and make it possible for party representatives to behave in a relatively consistent manner in interactions with voters (for a more detailed discussion of parliamentarians' thinking about following the party line, see Crowe 1983).[16] These factors may be useful to people who aspire to lead, but they may also act as a constraint when members want to speak their mind in public. We have seen on multiple occasions that potentially ambitious MPs truly believe it is important to express their personal convictions. The question is whether this has any impact when push comes to shove in plenary assembly votes.

The 1996 Parliamentary Study included a question that dealt with the MPs' usual voting behavior. Table 5.7 shows that potential career politicians report that

Table 5.7 MPs' voting behavior in the parliament

Potential career ambition	Breaks with the party line more often than others (%)
Yes	22
No	11
Difference	11**
Number of persons	277

Source: Parliamentary Study 1996.
Note: The survey question was, "If you think about votes in the Riksdag, would you say that you are among those who vote against the majority in your party more often than others, about as often, or less often?" *p < .1, **p < .05, ***p < .001.

they are more likely to *break with* the party line than are other MPs. Twice as many of them say they buck the party line more often than other MPs. The result is robust in a multivariate regression (logit).

Assuming that the ambitious MPs answered this question truthfully, the question that comes to mind is, why have they chosen such a risky strategy? Considering that potentially ambitious MPs have previously reported that they both talk more often and vote against their party more often, we might suspect that they belong to a category of "mavericks," that is, a category of MPs who go their own way.

The American research has noted a phenomenon referred to as the sacrificial lamb (Leuthold 1968).[17] A *sacrificial lamb* is a candidate who runs for election but has no chance of winning. The candidates' primary motivation is not to win the election but to bring attention to issues important to them or to their business (Canon 1990, 1993). Potentially ambitious MPs might be people whose strategic approach is limited to doing precisely as they wish. What contradicts such a thesis is that these MPs were in many cases already professional politicians when they were elected to the parliament for the first time. We are thus not dealing with political amateurs here. For this reason, it may be worthwhile to test whether potentially ambitious MPs, who certainly have a more provocative style, compensate for their behavior toward the party leadership in other contexts. Accordingly, we will now study whether potentially ambitious MPs play an "inside game" to strengthen their positions.

THE INSIDE GAME AND HOW TO GAIN INFLUENCE

If we presume that potentially ambitious MPs are engaged in an internal power play, what would such an "inside game" look like? The 1994 Parliamentary Study included questions about how MPs should behave to gain a hearing from their colleagues. Thanks to the Parliamentary Studies, it is possible to obtain a *direct* measure of what members should do to get their bills passed. The strategic considerations the MPs were queried about include aspects related to the internal power game: "opinion support within the party," "relations with the party leadership," and "debate at party group meetings."

In order to test whether there is an element of internal power play among potentially ambitious MPs, I have aggregated the three strategic considerations into an index. My intention is to test the extent to which the MPs ascribe significance to having "opinion support within the party," "winning debates at group meetings," and having good "relations with the party leadership." My goal is to find out whether potentially ambitious MPs assess the "inside game" differently than their colleagues and whether their tendencies to speak at group meetings and vote

Table 5.8 Do potentially ambitious MPs play an inside game? (OLS regression, standardized beta coefficients)

	Importance of the inside game
Career ambition	1.312**
Female	.098
Family background	−.014
Education	.831**
Age	−.042**
Professional politician	−.556*
Seniority	−.005
Status	−.501
Political party	
Center Party	−.110**
Christian Democratic Party	−.056
Conservative Party	−.057
Green Party	−.187
Left Party	−.143**
Liberal Party	−.187
R^2	.139
Number of persons	193

Sources: Parliamentary Study 1994, 1996.

Note: The survey question was, "In your experience, how important are the following factors in influencing decisions in your parliamentary group?" The response options were, "Very important," "Fairly important," "Fairly unimportant," and "Completely unimportant." The dependent variable is an index (0 to 10) based on the response options "Opinion support within the party," "Relations with the party leadership," and "Debate at group meetings." The independent variables are coded as follows: Career ambition: 0 = No career ambition, 1 = Career ambition; Female: 0 = Male, 1 = Female; Family background: 0 = Father blue-collar, 1 = Father small business owner or white-collar; Education: 0 = Not university educated, 1 = University educated; Occupation: 0 = Blue-collar, small business owner, and white-collar, 1 = Professional politician; Age: Serially according to age; Seniority: Serially by number of years in the parliament; Status: 0 = Have never held or have held a central party position, 1 = Have now a central party position. The Social Democratic Party is the reference category. *p < .1, **p < .05, ***p < .001. Alpha .713. Robust standard errors.

against their party can be explained by their strategic considerations. The results are shown in Table 5.8.

Looking at the table, we see that potentially ambitious MPs think it is important to be involved and to influence the inside game in order to have an impact. We can also see that professional politicians assess things differently than potentially ambitious MPs. An "education effect" also emerges. MPs with university education are more likely to emphasize the inside game to attain success. (The "outside game," in contrast, refers to having public opinion on your side and being on good terms with journalists; my findings showed no significant differences between potentially ambitious MPs and other MPs in their mastery of the outside game.)

In order to be certain that potentially ambitious MPs are engaging in an internal power play, the suggestions for how an MP should behave to gain influence are tested in various ways. The options the MPs could choose among were "opinion support in the party," "opinion support among the electorate as a whole," "relations with the mass media," "relations with the party leadership," debate at group meetings," "connections with other parties," "support of concerned organizations/government agencies," and "expert/specialist support."

Another possibility is that potentially ambitious MPs take a broad approach and cultivate relationships with many different stakeholders. For this reason, all of the options were aggregated into an index and tested in a multivariate regression analysis. The test showed that MPs with career ambitions are no more likely than others to invest in a wide range of contacts. Instead, potentially ambitious MPs have a clearly discernible strategic approach aimed at party-internal relationships. The really big difference between potentially ambitious MPs and other MPs has to do with how they estimate the importance of opinion support within their own parties. The difference is 20 percentage points between the two groups of MPs. Among potentially ambitious MPs, 74 percent think opinion support within their own party is very important; just over half the other MPs share that assessment. When it comes to relations with the party leadership, 21 percent of potentially ambitious MPs think they are very important. Of the other MPs, 14 percent make the same estimation.[18]

If we instead attempt to find factors indicating that MPs truly do not believe in the strategy of cultivating good relations with the party leadership, we must look among the professional politicians—who do not have potential career ambitions. Among this group, 3 percent consider it very important to have good relations with the party leadership. When we compare this figure with the MPs in the same group who do have potential career ambitions, we see a noticeable gap: among the ambitious, 25 percent of the professional politicians think it is very important to have good relations with the party leadership. Taken as a whole, this provides strong support for the notion that potentially ambitious MPs engage in strategic behavior aimed at party-internal conditions that also differ from the estimations of other MPs.

RELATIONS WITH PARTY LEADERSHIP

Based on the arguments surrounding the inside game, it has emerged that both voting behavior and behavior in discussions at party group meetings can be linked to the MPs' strategic approach. What remains is an attempt to relate the MPs' stra-

Table 5.9 Do ambitious MPs consider the party leadership when they make decisions? (OLS regression, standardized beta coefficients)

	MPs state the extent to which they take the party leadership into account when they make decisions
Career ambition	.139*
Female	–.048
Family background	–.126
Education	.037
Age	–.378***
Professional politician	–.002
Seniority	.046
Status	.015
Political party	
Center Party	.138**
Christian Democratic Party	.111*
Conservative Party	–.185*
Green Party	.028
Left Party	.070
Liberal Party	–.149*
Pseudo R^2	.216
Number of persons	196

Source: Parliamentary Study 1996.
Note: The survey question was, "How much consideration do you give to the opinion of each of the following groups when you make political decisions?" The response option that constitutes the dependent variable was, "Party leadership." The scale was from 1 = "Great consideration" to 7 = "Very little consideration." The scale has been reversed in the regression table. The independent variables are coded as follows: Career ambition: 0 = No career ambition, 1 = Career ambition; Female: 0 = Male, 1 = Female; Family background: 0 = Father blue-collar, 1 = Father small business owner or white-collar; Education: 0 = Not university educated, 1 = University educated; Occupation: 0 = Blue-collar, small business owner, and white collar, 1 = Professional politician; Age: Serially according to age; Seniority: Serially by number of years in the parliament; Status: 0 = Have never held or have held a central party position, 1 = Have now a central party position. The Social Democratic Party is the reference category. $*p < .1$, $**p < .05$, $***p < .001$. Robust standard errors.

tegic assessments of the inside game to their relations with the party leadership. The importance of having good relations with the party leadership might be one explanation for why potentially ambitious MPs have the courage to stand out from the crowd. Quite simply, they are counting on compensating for their voting behavior and behavior at group meetings with good relations with the party leadership.

The 1996 Parliamentary Study asked MPs what they consider when they make political decisions. The categories included the party leadership. The idea is thus that potentially ambitious MPs balance their more "questionable" conduct in connection with party votes by being more amenable to the party leadership in other contexts. Accordingly, I tested whether it is also possible to link the MPs' strategic assessments of the inside game to the party leadership with regard to what the MPs usually consider when they make their decisions. The results are presented in Table 5.9.

The table shows that potentially ambitious MPs say that they give greater consideration to the party leadership when they must make political decisions. This strategic approach seems to gain support when the MPs describe their day-to-day work in the parliament.[19] These results thus strengthen the impression that there is a relation between potentially ambitious MPs and strategic behavior. The MPs are quite simply not a breed of "mavericks" who always go their own way; instead, their behavior is in harmony with what the MPs consider strategically important to gaining influence.

We have mainly studied circumstances that touch upon the party and parliamentary arena, and it may be interesting to conclude this section by testing the notion that MPs with career ambitions generally strive to achieve good strategic conditions for fulfilling their aspirations. The survey material from 1996 contains various suggestions concerning political issues upon which the MPs could take a stance. One of the questions has to do with whether the MPs favored or opposed gender quotas for state and municipal managerial positions. Based on the state of the current system, more men than women hold the top jobs (Swedish Government Report [SOU] 2007:108). It's generally accepted that gender quotas are advantageous to women and disadvantageous to men, including women and men in state and municipal managerial positions. If we test the proposition that male MPs with career ambitions should be more likely to oppose the idea than other men and that women with similar ambitions should be less averse to gender quotas than other women, what happens?

Table 5.10 shows the percentage of MPs who believe that gender quotas for state and municipal positions are a "Very bad idea." The MPs are categorized according to gender and potential career ambitions.

If one can see the question about gender quotas for top managerial positions as a kind of measure of strategic interest, the results presented in the table tell us that those who plan to climb in the political hierarchy favor or disfavor the idea depending on how it would affect their potential for career attainment. The difference between men and women who have reported that they aspire to influential positions is 57 percentage points whereas the corresponding difference between men and women who have no such aspirations is only 16 percentage points. In other words, there is a significantly greater difference between men and women who are seeking political influence.

Generally speaking, more men than women think gender quotas are a bad

Table 5.10 MPs who think gender quotas for executive positions in state and municipal organizations are a very bad idea

	Potential career ambitions (%)	Without potential career ambitions (%)	Difference (%)
Male	63	36	27****
Female	6	20	14
Difference	57***	16***	

Source: Parliamentary Study 1996.
Note: The question was, "The following list covers a number of suggestions that have been made in political debate. What is your opinion about each of them? Gender quotas in state and municipal organizations (top managerial positions)." The response options were, "Very good idea," "Fairly good idea," "Neither a good idea nor a bad idea," "Fairly bad idea," and "Very bad idea." *p < .1, **p < .05, ***p < .001.

idea—but there is a pattern here, as well. Women who do not have potential career ambitions are three times more likely to think gender quotas are a very bad idea, but the difference is not significant. Male potentially ambitious MPs dislike the idea of female gender quotas more than other men do—almost two-thirds of the former think it is a very bad idea. Men who say they do not have career ambitions do not have the same strong preferences. The main impression of the MPs' strategic assessments is thus that they are not confined to that which occurs in and around the parliament. If we can believe in earnest that self-interest never lies, this would constitute additional evidence that the simple measurement used in the survey measures a phenomenon that can be related to career ambition.

Potentially ambitious MPs appear to have a certain self-interest attached to their career opportunities. Let us therefore take a brief look at their attitudes toward influence and status.

MPS' CAREER AMBITIONS AND ATTITUDES TOWARD HIGH-STATUS POSITIONS

In the 1994 Parliamentary Study questions were asked that concerned how much power and influence various actors/institutions and positions then had. The question about institutions identified the government, the parliament, the political parties, and the electorate. These four institutions can be said to constitute the political system within which the MPs act. If we merge these four institutions to an index and study the MPs' attitudes toward how much influence the current (1994) political system has, we can see certain differences that have to do with potential career ambition.

Table 5.11 MPs' estimation of the power and influence of the current political system (OLS regression, standardized beta coefficients)

	The political system's current influence
Career ambition	.186**
Female	.052
Family background	–.044
Education	–.084
Age	–.212**
Professional politician	–.037
Seniority	.031
Status	–.050
Political party	
Center Party	.039
Christian Democratic Party	–.008
Conservative Party	.028
Green Party	–.176***
Left Party	.101
Liberal Party	.112
R^2	.139
Number of persons	178

Sources: Parliamentary Study 1994, 1996.

Note: The survey question was, "Based on the scale below, please indicate how much influence each of the listed organizations has on Swedish society today, and how much influence you believe each should have on Swedish society today." The scale was from 0 to 10. The index includes the parliament, the government, the political parties, and the electorate. The independent variables are coded as follows: Career ambition: 0 = No career ambition, 1 = Career ambition; Female: 0 = Male, 1 = Female; Family background: 0 = Father blue-collar, 1 = Father small business owner or white-collar; Education: 0 = Not university educated, 1 = University educated; Occupation: 0 = Blue-collar, small business owner, and white-collar, 1 = Professional politician; Age: Serially according to age; Seniority: Serially by number of years in the parliament; Status: 0 = Have never held or have held a central party position, 1 = Have now a central party position. The Social Democratic Party is the reference category. *$p < .1$, **$p < .05$, ***$p < .001$. Alpha .702. Robust standard errors.

Potentially ambitious MPs believe to a higher extent than their colleagues that the current political system has great influence on society. Table 5.11 also shows that older MPs have more faith in the current influence of the political system. The pessimists are found among the MPs from the Green Party. This might not come as a surprise. The Green Party was at this time not established in the parliament and perhaps had not experienced the influence the political system actually can have on developments in society.

Based on the results shown in this table, we can surmise that potentially ambitious MPs' faith in the political system is connected to the fact that they also

Table 5.12 MPs' estimation of the status of various political positions (OLS regression, standardized beta coefficients)

	Status ascribed to various political positions by MPs
Career ambition	.051
Female	.283***
Family background	−.206**
Education	−.010
Age	−.138
Professional politician	−.206**
Seniority	−.019
Status	−.097
Political party	
Center Party	.037
Christian Democratic Party	−.015
Conservative Party	.166*
Green Party	−.157**
Left Party	−.105*
Liberal Party	−.034
R^2	.248
Number of persons	189

Sources: Parliamentary Study 1994, 1996.

Note: The survey question was, "How much status/prestige do you believe the following offices and positions have among MPs in general?" The MPs were allowed to rank the positions on a scale from 0 to 10. The positions included in the index are ambassador, party whip, county governor, member of the party group, member of the national party board of directors, cabinet minister, speaker of the parliament, and committee chair. The independent variables are coded as follows: Career ambition: 0 = No career ambition, 1 = Career ambition; Female: 0 = Male, 1 = Female; Family background: 0 = Father blue-collar, 1 = Father small business owner or white-collar; Education: 0 = Not university educated, 1 = University educated; Occupation: 0 = Blue-collar, small business owner, and white-collar, 1 = Professional politician; Age: Serially according to age; Seniority: Serially by number of years in the parliament; Status: 0 = Have never held or have held a central party position, 1 = Have now a central party position. The Social Democratic Party is the reference category. *$p < .1$, **$p < .05$, ***$p < .001$. Robust standard errors.

ascribe great power and prestige to the top positions in that system. It would make sense to assume that one reason for the faith in the influence of the political system is related to personal ambition. But such is not the case. The 1994 Parliamentary Study also included questions that allowed the MPs to rank the status of various political positions on a scale of 0 to 10. A number of prominent positions were included on the list; I use these in the next chapter as the basis for assessing the MPs' career attainment. These positions are ambassador, party group leader, county governor, member of the parliament party group, member of the national party board, cabinet minister, speaker of the parliament, and committee chair. If we use these positions to construct a "status index" in order to study whether potentially ambitious MPs ascribe higher status to these positions than do other MPs, we see that potentially ambitious MPs do not differentiate themselves. The results are shown in Table 5.12.

Potentially ambitious MPs are not enthralled with the status of the positions per se. If we more specifically study the status of the position of cabinet minister, for example, potentially ambitious MPs give the position an average score of 9.02 on a scale of 0 to 10. Other MPs give the position of cabinet minister a score of 9.11. It is thus not entirely clear that we can put an equal sign between potential career ambition and status-seeking. (However, the more general assumption that there is a correlation between faith in the influence of the political system and the status of the positions is correct. When the index for faith in the current political system is included in the regression model from Table 5.12, a statistically significant correlation emerges between the estimation of the status of top positions and the influence of the political system. At least in this sense, status and influence are connected.)

Table 5.12 reveals that MPs whose backgrounds are such that they have historically had a longer route to these positions ascribe them higher status. The people who believe these positions carry high status are women and MPs from blue-collar homes, as well as MPs who are not professional politicians. Perhaps a high-status position can be likened to money—those who do not have it value it the most.

THERE ARE MPS WITH REAL CAREER AMBITIONS

The time has come to gather the impressions. The question was whether it is possible to find any correlation between potentially ambitious MPs and certain behavior. In other words, we were going to test whether career ambition can constitute an explanation for what happens in and around the parliament. We compared two scenarios. In the first, ambitious MPs are described as people who are close to the party leadership and are cautious about standing out or making a fuss. In the second scenario, ambitious MPs are people who cultivate a personal reputation and want all eyes on them.

There was also awareness that neither alternative was necessarily accurate and thus would not meet the criterion that ambitious MPs must behave a particular way. The results clearly showed, however, that the operationalization of career ambition relates to strategic behavior. The simple measurement used to measure career ambition seems able to pick up an aspect that can be linked specifically to ambitious MPs.

Ambitious MPs want to make a personal mark in the role of elected representative. They consider it important to represent their own convictions; representing their constituencies or individual voters is secondary. But the MPs do not ignore their constituencies—they focus their attention on the constituency during election campaigns in order to be reelected.

When it comes to their relationship to the party, we could discern that these MPs are not putty in the hands of the party leadership. The MPs act strategically and play an inside game. They set themselves apart in reporting that they challenge the party leadership in certain contexts and vote against their party more often than others, and are eager to speak out at party group meetings. They compensate for their more provocative style by bowing to the leadership in other contexts.

There are also clear indications that these MPs harbor a certain self-interest with regard to structural circumstances. Women who want to climb the career ladder are distinctly more favorable toward gender quotas than are men with career ambitions. The interpretation is thus that MPs who are intent on a career want to be in an environment as facilitative as possible for their career endeavors.

In the preceding chapter we determined that the politicians who reported aspirations to advance in the political system came from higher-resource backgrounds. This chapter has clarified that ambitious MPs are a group who emphasize their own convictions, speak out often, and have the courage to challenge the party leadership. Individuals aiming for career attainment thus seem to have the self-confidence that can be logically associated with the ambitious. The results are perhaps no great surprise, but they are quite expressive of the effectiveness of the measurement used, as it identifies a phenomenon that can be linked to ambitious MPs. Potential career politicians are not merely potential career politicians: in this respect they are politicians with real career ambitions.

To test whether the established definition is solid, I have studied the MPs who are interested only in a career in the parliament. What I wanted to know was whether the MPs who only want a career in the parliament resemble MPs aiming for a political career beyond the parliament. If great similarities were found between these groups, it would have been evidence that the established definition needed to be modified. But such is not the case.

We'll now look at a number of examples indicating that the MPs categorized as politicians with career ambitions differ from MPs who only want to advance in the parliament. If we specifically study MPs only interested in a career in the parliament, we discover they are people who are *not* professional politicians and who joined their parties later in life. The MPs who fit the definition of politicians with career ambitions, in comparison, entered politics in their youth and are often professional politicians. In other words, professional politicians as a group differ significantly regardless of which definition is used—but in *different* directions.

When it comes to activities in the parliament, it emerges that 27 percent of the MPs who only want a career in the parliament think it is *very important* to represent their own political convictions, which may be compared to 51 percent among those who have career ambitions according to the accepted definition. Moreover, among those who want a career in the parliament, only 3 percent report that they break with the party line *more often* than others. This differs considerably from the MPs with "real" career ambitions, of whom 22 percent report that they break with the party line more often than others. Nearly half of the ambitious MPs (43 percent) report that they speak out at parliamentary group meetings *almost every time.* The corresponding figure for those who want only a career in the parliament is 27 percent. In addition, 50 percent of ambitious MPs are *very* interested in international issues in general, which may be compared to the 21 percent among MPs who want a career in the parliament. Going back to Chapter 4, we can also remind ourselves that MPs who only want a career in the parliament are found primarily among first-term MPs and that MPs who have sat in the parliament for more than one term are not nearly as interested in a career in the parliament. The corresponding tendency was not found among the ambitious MPs. MPs who only want a career in the parliament do not generally differ from other parliamentarians and do not resemble the MPs who intend to carve out a political career outside the parliament. It would thus have been misleading to fail to differentiate between MPs who want to move to a higher-status institution from those who only want a career in the parliament. This strengthens the impression that the definition used in the book applies to ambitious MPs and that aspirations to move to another institution are central to the discussion of politicians with career ambitions. The result also strengthens the findings in the American context. Rebekah Herrick and Michael Moore (1993) have earlier stressed the importance of differentiating between intra-institutional ambitions and progressive ambitions.

At any rate, the collective affinity may be strong in the parliament, but MPs who want to advance in the political system give themselves ample room to maneuver. In the next chapter we will more closely study the extent to which their strategic behavior is successful. How have things progressed for the MPs who said they aspired to career attainment after ten years? Have they succeeded at their endeavors?

6. Are Ambitious MPs Successful?

We now know there are ambitious politicians in the parliament. Two questions remain. On the one hand, I want to know whether ambitious MPs achieve career attainment. My question is simple: Does the drive to make a career in politics lead to career attainment? On the other hand, I want to put the Swedish results in a comparative light: Does Sweden differ from other European parliaments with regard to the occurrence of ambitious MPs? We will discuss the first question in this chapter. Chapter 7 will report on the proportion of MPs in European parliaments who have career ambitions.

AMBITION AND CAREER ATTAINMENT

The research on which MPs achieve successful careers in legislative assemblies is relatively limited (Patzelt 1999). Scholars have instead studied who gets elected to parliament and the consequences (Esaiasson and Holmberg 1996; Eulau and Wahlke 1978; Holmberg 1974; Kavanagh 1992; Norris 1996, 1997; Norris and Lovenduski 1995; Putnam 1976).

Because they presume that everyone who runs for office is ambitious, American researchers are more interested in which strategies are successful than in which legislative members succeed in their careers (see, e.g., Banks and Kiewiet 1989; Gaddie and Bullock 2000; Jacobson 1989; Jacobson and Kernell 1983; Maisel and Stone 1997; Mayhew 1974; Squire 1989; Wrighton and Squire 1997). In the European context, there is to the best of my knowledge only one study that has more rigorously examined the relationship between MPs' motivations and career attainment, Stuart Elaine Macdonald's 1987 doctoral dissertation, *Political Ambition and Attainment: A Dynamic Analysis of Parliamentary Careers*. Macdonald was a member of Donald Searing's research team, which had undertaken a major study of British parliamentarians in the 1970s.[1] In that context, MPs were queried about their career ambitions. Thirteen years later, Macdonald analyzed how the respondents' careers had developed. The results showed that the MPs who reported political ambitions had been more successful than others (Macdonald 1987). There is a problem with Macdonald's study, however: the operationalization of ambition was based upon two things—which offices the members aspired to, and how the members assessed their chances of succeeding. The variable ran between 0 and 9. MPs who aspired to become cabinet ministers and believed their chances were good were assigned a score of 9. MPs who aspired to become cabinet ministers but assessed their chances as slight were given the value of 0. MPs who said they aspired to become cabinet ministers and believed that their opportunities were limited were thus given the same score as MPs who were not at all interested in the office (ibid). The hope for career attainment thus did not suffice to be regarded as an ambitious MP—the MP also had to believe his or her chances of success were good. This introduces the suspicion that Macdonald's results over-interpret the importance of ambition.

DO THEIR AMBITIONS HAVE ANY IMPACT ON THE MPS' CAREERS?

The main question is whether the MPs' career trajectory between 1996 and 2006 has any relationship to their career ambitions. What I am interested in is whether the ambition to advance in the political system within a ten-year period reflects an actual career trajectory. If there is such a relationship, it would prove that career ambition has long-term significance, which has an impact when it comes to which MPs hold the top positions in our parliamentary system.

The MPs' careers will be examined from more than one perspective. A career may, for example, start at different points in time and proceed at different rates. Therefore, the first thing I want to know is whether ambitious MPs began their parliamentary careers earlier than others and how soon after joining their parties they were elected to the parliament. Thus, the focus here is on the "speed" of the career trajectory.

The second aspect I will study is the MPs' ability to fulfill their short-term preferences. Although career ambition is a long-term proposition, we can study whether ambition becomes manifest in relation to positions in the near future. I do this by looking at the MPs' ability to attain seats on the committees they prefer.

The third perspective is preoccupied with the question of whether ambitious MPs are better than others at retaining their seats in parliament. There were three general elections between 1996 and 2006. The MPs must survive internal party nominations and the voters' verdict, as well as avoid political scandals. Do ambitious MPs perform better, or worse, than other MPs in this respect? After considering this question the chapter will conclude by looking at whether ambitious MPs also experience career attainment over time.

In order to discover what role ambition plays in the MPs' career trajectories, three main scenarios can be actualized. Career ambition may either have a positive or a negative impact on political career attainment. Positive impacts would include a faster route to the parliament, superior attainment of interim goals, successful retention of seats in parliament, and that the ambitious MPs' careers are going better than those of other MPs.

The same applies, albeit in the reverse, to the negative impacts that ambition may have on career attainment: it takes longer to make it to the parliament, the MPs do not attain their interim goals, they do not retain their seats, and their careers develop less well than those of other MPs. The results may also show something else entirely—that the career as such is not affected by the MPs' career ambitions. In such a case, the ambition to achieve career attainment is quite simply of negligible importance to the MPs' actual career attainments.

MPS' CAPACITY TO REACH THE PARLIAMENT AT AN EARLY AGE

It is possible that ambitious MPs already have experience of successful advancement in the political system by the time they are first elected to parliament. One such sign might be that ambitious MPs distinguish themselves on the path to parliament by arriving there faster than others.

In order to test the MPs' "speed" in getting into the parliament, we will study two different aspects: how many years it took the MPs to arrive in the parliament after they joined their parties, and how old they were when elected to the parliament for the first time. I want to know whether the MPs who aspire to advance in the political system take a long-term approach, not only in the sense that they are willing to go after positions further in the future but also whether we can trace a long-term approach retrospectively in the sense that they achieved their parliamentary office earlier and/or more quickly than others.

The data shows that the average age at which ambitious MPs entered the parliament is thirty-nine, compared to forty-three for the other MPs. There is thus a difference of four years between the two groups. We also see a difference when we look at how long it took for the MPs to get to the parliament after they joined their parties. Ambitious MPs make it to the parliament somewhat faster than others. On average, it took them sixteen years to get to parliament and took the others an additional two years. This difference, however, is not primarily dependent upon the MPs' career ambitions, as shown in Table 6.1.

Ambitious MPs do not have a shorter path to parliament from party membership to election to the parliament.[2] Those who have the shortest route are women, the highly educated, and MPs who did not grow up in blue-collar homes. It takes a little more than fourteen years for a university-educated woman who did not grow up in a blue-collar home to make it to the parliament, but about twenty-two years for a man with no university education from a blue-collar background.[3]

Table 6.1 MPs' swiftness to the parliament with regard to age and years of party membership (OLS regression, standardized b coefficients)

	Number of years from party membership to the parliament	MP's age upon first election in the parliament
Career ambition	.057	−.120**
Female	−.189**	.090
Family background	−.125*	−.072
Education	−.214**	−.109
Professional politician	−.003	−.083
Status	.039	−.057
Political party		
Center Party	−.002	.154**
Christian Democratic Party	.024	.192*
Conservative Party	.153**	.258**
Green Party	−.221***	.173*
Left Party	−.039	.160**
Liberal Party	.075	.124*
R^2	.218	.127
Number of persons	202	204

Sources: Parliamentary Study 1994, 1996.
Note: The first dependent variable is constructed by subtracting the year the MP was first elected to the Riksdag from the year the MP reported joining the party. The other dependent variable is constructed by subtracting the MP's age from the year the MP was elected to the parliament. The independent variables are coded as follows: Career ambition: 0 = No career ambition, 1 = Career ambition; Female: 0 = Male, 1 = Female; Family background: 0 = Father blue-collar, 1 = Father small business owner or white-collar; Education: 0 = Not university educated, 1 = University educated; Occupation: 0 = Blue-collar, small business owner, and white-collar, 1 = Professional politician; Age: Serially according to age; Seniority: Serially by number of years in the parliament; Status: 0 = Have never held or have held a central party position, 1 = Have now a central party position. The Social Democratic Party is the reference category. *p < .1, **p < .05, ***p < .001. Robust standard errors.

With regard to women's shorter route to politics, it should be noted that the 1994–1998 term of office was a bit unusual. An activist group who called themselves the "Support Stockings" expressed discontent with how the established parties were working with issues that impinged on the condition of women in society. In the preceding term of office (1991–1994), the proportion of women in the parliament had declined to 33 percent. In response, activists exhorted the parties to alternate their ballot lists according to "every other name a woman" principle. Representatives of the Support Stockings threatened to form their own party if the parliamentary parties did not mend their ways. The parties bowed to the demands to a varying degree (Freidenvall 2006). The result was that the proportion of women in the parliament rose above 40 percent. For this reason, the figures presented here may be somewhat distorted. Women's faster route to the parliament may quite simply have been hastened by the external pressure that existed at the time. Research has shown, however, that at the local government level women have a faster route to their first office than do men (Karlsson 2001). Women's route to the parliament is thus probably shorter than the men's, but perhaps not quite as short as it would appear according to the data in Table 6.1.[4]

Ambitious MPs are younger than their colleagues when they become MPs. The same applies to MPs from the Social Democrats. Social Democratic MPs are about forty when they enter the parliament for the first time and are younger than MPs from the other parties. The oldest MPs upon first election to the parliament are Center Party representatives, who are on average forty-four when they enter the parliament. If we relate the age of MPs to their parliamentary debut and career attainment, we can confirm that no Swedish prime minister since World War II has been older than thirty-four when first elected to the parliament.[5] This suggests that MPs who end up high in the political hierarchy also became MPs at a relatively early age.

MPS' CAPACITY TO FULFILL THEIR SHORT-TERM PREFERENCES

The definition of career ambition presumes that the MPs must be goal-oriented, but it is unclear whether this attribute has any impact on how well the MPs are able to fulfill their short-term preferences. In this case, the capacity to fulfill short-term preferences has to do with the extent to which ambitious MPs have seats on their preferred committees. The parliamentary committees in the parliament constitute a key resource for MPs who are seeking influence (Esaiasson and Holmberg 1996:230; Hagevi 1998:238ff).

In his thesis, political scientist Magnus Hagevi (1998) has shown that MPs have some room for negotiation in connection with committee assignments. The MPs' own preferences are strongly considered when seats are allocated, and the party leaderships cannot do as they please when filling committee seats (ibid., 213ff). Perhaps the MPs' career ambitions give their preferences greater impact—but they may also "expose" the MPs and make them less successful than their colleagues.

Hagevi (ibid., chapter 5) has shown that the three most desirable committees are Finance, Trade and Industry, and Foreign Affairs. Table 6.2 presents the percentage of ambitious and nonambitious politicians who would prefer to sit on the three most popular committees.

Table 6.2 MPs' most preferred committees

Career ambitions	Finance (%)	Trade and Industry (%)	Foreign Affairs (%)	Total
Yes	21	14	12	47
No	13	11	7	31

Sources: Parliamentary Study 1994, 1996.
Note: The survey question was: "If you had your choice, on which committee would you prefer to be a standing member?" (*N* = 237).

Almost half the ambitious MPs prefer to sit on the most desirable committees whereas the other MPs are more fragmented in their preferences. Among the MPs that do not have career ambitions, only about one-third would prefer to serve on one of these committees. If we aggregate the three most popular committees in order to study which MPs aspire to them, the differences are significant in a multivariate regression analysis. To a higher extent than others, ambitious MPs want to sit on the most popular committees and thus expose themselves to greater competition when it comes to fulfilling their preferences.

The committees are also related to status. The Finance Committee and the Trade and Industry Committee are, according to the MPs, two of the most powerful and prestigious. The Constitutional Committee is a third prestigious committee (Hagevi 1998, chapter 3). When we aggregate the Finance, Foreign Affairs, and Constitutional Committees into a common status category in order to test whether ambitious MPs seek power and prestige, however, no such tendencies appear. The results can be said to repeat the results presented in Chapter 5, which showed that ambitious MPs are not more status-oriented than other MPs. Ambitious MPs want to sit on the most popular committees, not those with the highest status.

Are ambitious MPs good at acquiring seats on the committees where they personally want to serve? To find out, we will compare their preferred committees to the committees on which the MPs actually serve. If in this context we study what proportion of the ambitious MPs are found on the three most popular committees, we can confirm that they are overrepresented. By *overrepresented* I mean that 29 percent of ambitious MPs are found in the Finance, Trade and Industry, or Foreign Affairs Committees, even though as a group they constitute only 18 percent of all MPs. This does not, however, mean that ambitious MPs are better at acquiring seats on "their" committees, as shown by the results of a multivariate analysis presented in Table 6.3.

Ambitious MPs are neither better nor worse at fulfilling their short-term preferences. Goal orientation with regard to their personal careers thus has no effect. A majority (56 percent) of ambitious MPs sit on their preferred committees. The corresponding figure for MPs who do not have career ambitions is 59 percent. The

Table 6.3 MPs' capacity to attain seats on their preferred committees (logit regression, odds ratio)

Career ambition	.681
Female	1.306
Family background	1.919
Education	.723
Age	1.017
Professional politician	.742
Seniority	1.104**
Status	3.580**
Political party	
Center Party	.297*
Christian Democratic Party	.657
Conservative Party	1.226
Green Party	.453
Left Party	.730
Liberal Party	.283**
Pseudo R^2	.121
Number of persons	191

Sources: Parliamentary Study 1994, 1996.
Note: The dependent variable is binary, 0–1. The MPs who sit on their preferred committees are assigned the value of 1. MPs who would prefer to sit on another committee have been assigned the value of 0. The independent variables are coded as follows: Career ambition: 0 = No career ambition, 1 = Career ambition; Female: 0 = Male, 1 = Female; Family background: 0 = Father blue-collar, 1 = Father small business owner or white-collar; Education: 0 = Not university educated, 1 = University educated; Occupation: 0 = Blue-collar, small business owner, and white-collar, 1 = Professional politician; Age: Serially according to age; Seniority: Serially by number of years in the parliament; Status: 0 = Have never held or have held a central party position, 1 = Have now a central party position. The Social Democratic Party is the reference category. *$p < .1$, **$p < .05$, ***$p < .001$. Robust standard errors.

MPs who have best succeeded at fulfilling their preferences are those who have served the longest in the parliament, are prominent figures in the party organization, and are members of one of the two large parties. In other words, ambition is not a deciding factor in how successful the MPs are at acquiring seats on their most preferred committees.

MPS' CAPACITY TO RETAIN THEIR SEATS IN THE PARLIAMENT

At the beginning of the book, we had a taste of how Swedish politicians tend to shy away from talking about their own career ambitions. When Prime Minister Göran Persson was asked whether he had ever aspired to be the party leader, his answer was that this was frowned upon. The law of the land is "He who wants to be chosen seldom is" (Göran Persson on the Swedish television program *Uppdrag Granskning*, 1998) and "that kind of careerism is detected and then you are culled" (Madestam 2009:97).

The consequence of expressing a wish for an office or a position may thus be failure to attain it. If this is true, ambition is a barrier to a successful political career. The drive to achieve career attainment may lead to discord and conflict within the parties. The longest serving prime minister of Sweden, Tage Erlander, for example, described in his diaries how minister of social affairs Gustav Möller, after having seen himself passed over in the election of the party leader, made his discontent with the party known in various ways. For example, Möller repeatedly made statements that put the Social Democratic leadership in awkward positions (Erlander 2001).[6] All things considered, it seems important to ask whether ambitious MPs are forced to leave the parliament involuntarily more often than others. I will thus not only find out which MPs are still in the parliament but also study whether the MPs have voluntarily or involuntarily vacated their seats in parliament and whether those who have voluntarily or involuntarily left are the more successful MPs or the less successful.

BASIS OF CALCULATING THE MPS' CAREER ATTAINMENT

Before we can come to grips with assessing the MPs' careers, we need a way to measure the MPs' career attainment—but there is no obvious way to construct a career attainment index. As an example, in Peter Esaiasson and Sören Holmberg's 1996 study *Representation from Above,* the MPs' career score was distributed between 0 and 2, depending on the positions the MPs held. In *Exit Riksdagen,* which studied the causes behind the increasing numbers of MPs leaving the parliament, no distinction was made as to the status of the various political positions. Instead, each position was given one point for each year the MP held the position (Ahlbäck Öberg, Hermansson, and Wängnerud 2007:41).

The scoring system used in this book makes an attempt to include the MPs' own estimations of which political positions carry status. In the 1994 Parliamentary Study, the MPs were able to rank various political positions according to their level of prestige (see Chapter 5). The MPs were presented with eighteen political positions, which they could score between 0 and 10. The average score for the eighteen positions was 6.2. Seven positions had an average score above 6.2. These seven positions were cabinet minister, committee chair, party group leader, member of the party's national council, speaker of the parliament, ambassador, and county governor. Accordingly, all positions that received a score above 6.2 are included among the political positions in the construction of the index. These positions are joined by the positions covered in *Exit Riksdagen*: deputy speaker, deputy chair of a committee, party leader, and party secretary. Added to these are positions in the EU organization, which all received a status score above 6.2. There is always an argument to be made that there should be more or fewer positions included in the calculation system, and as to whether there are positions included that should have been omitted, and vice versa.

I have, however, developed various calculation systems that incorporate both fewer and more positions, but there was no effect on the main result. In other words, the results do not depend on exactly which positions are included.[7]

Nevertheless, a selection must be made. My selection criteria were thus based on what other scholars have previously done, as well as an attempt to "eavesdrop" on the MPs' own estimations. The scoring system goes from 1 to 3. The political positions that the MPs gave a score of 8 or above are assigned 3 points (cabinet minister, speaker of the parliament, and EU commissioner), to which is added the position of party leader (taken from *Exit Riksdagen*). It is relatively easy to see that these positions have higher status than the position of director-general of a state agency, for example. Political positions with an average score between 7 and 8 are assigned 2 points in the calculation system (party group leader, committee chair, and ambassador). These positions are augmented by the position of party secretary (taken from *Exit Riksdagen*).

Positions given an average score below 7 but above 6.2—county governor, member of the party's national council, and director-general—are assigned 1 point. The group given 1 point also includes deputy committee chair, deputy speaker (taken from *Exit Riksdagen*), and positions within the EU parliament.

WHICH MPS REMAIN IN THE PARLIAMENT FOR THE 2006–2010 TERM?

The proportion of MPs retained after general elections has declined over the years. Presently, about 30 percent of MPs are replaced at every election (Ahlbäck Öberg, Hermansson, and Wängnerud 2007). This means that we should expect about

Table 6.4 Proportion of MPs still in the parliament after ten years

Career ambitions	Remaining after 10 years (%)
Yes	33
No	14
Difference	19***

Sources: Parliamentary Study 1996; Fakta om folkvalda, Riksdagen 2006–2010.
Note: The data on how many MPs remain are based on a comparison between the MPs who participated in the 1996 survey and the MPs elected to the Riksdag in 2006. *p < .1, **p < .05, ***p < .001.

one-third of the MPs who responded to the 1996 survey to still be in office for the 2006–2010 term. The MPs, however, did harbor some optimism about their futures. In the 1996 survey, 40 percent reported that they intended to still be in office in ten years, but considerably fewer succeeded. If we study how many of the MPs who participated in the 1996 study were still in the parliament at the beginning of the 2006–2010 term, we find only 18 percent. This means that fewer than half of those who aspired to retain their seats in the Riksdag held on and succeeded in their endeavors. How, then, have things gone for ambitious MPs? Table 6.4 shows that ambitious MPs actually did retain their seats to a higher extent.

A larger proportion of the ambitious MPs are still in the parliament after ten years. The difference is close to 20 percentage points.[8] It is apparent, though, that career ambition is no guarantee that MPs will successfully retain their seats. Above two-thirds of the MPs with career ambitions have been eliminated from parliament. Career ambition has no significant effect on whether MPs retain their seats in the parliament in a multiregression analyses. In the main, it is the more obvious factors like age and tenure in the parliament that have an impact.

Over the years, career-minded MPs have not been better at retaining their seats in the parliament despite their ambitions and their strategic behavior. In other words, the career motivation is not enough to guarantee that MPs will survive first the internal partisan political game and then the voters' judgment on election day. The next question thus becomes what has happened to these MPs during this period of time; that is, how have ambitious MPs been removed from their seats in the parliament?

To find out why the MPs left office, each MP who is no longer in the parliament was traced using three search engines, Mediearkivet, Presstext, and Google, and through the Swedish Election Authority's website. I began by using the search engines to try to discover whether there were any controversies involved and/or whether the MPs themselves have talked about why they are no longer in the parliament.

In the analysis that follows, the reasons for the exits have been reduced to two: voluntary and involuntary. The voluntary group includes all MPs who ahead of a general election announced that they intended to leave office, as well as those who were not embroiled in a conflict with their parties when they stepped down. The same applies to MPs who left office before the end of the term to accept a job offer. The involuntary group includes all MPs who were forced to resign due to scandals or protests, were dropped by the party to an unelectable place on the candidate list, lost a preference vote, or were eliminated when the party lost a seat. Data from the Election Authority were used to check which MPs lost a preference vote. Ballots from the various general elections are available on the Election Authority's website, which makes it possible to check whether the MP was on the ballot and whether he or she lost the seat by losing a preference vote or whether the party itself made a poor showing.

It is naturally difficult to preclude that some of the MPs who left voluntarily have not done so because they lacked party support. The impression after reading hundreds of newspaper articles is that such MPs make it known if they feel they were treated unfairly, or else the newspapers report conflicts within the party. This impression is strengthened by the checks I was able to perform by means of access to the material from the study of MPs who have left the parliament, *Exit Riksdagen*. In that study, MPs were afforded the opportunity to report why they were no longer in the parliament. One of the response options was that the MP had not been nominated by his or her party. When the survey data were compared to the information derived from the search engines, it emerged that the MPs who stated in the *Exit Riksdagen* study that they had not been nominated had also figured in media discussions.

WHY HAVE THE MPS LEFT THE PARLIAMENT?

Two regression models are shown on Table 6.5. The first of these tests the relationship between various explanatory factors and MPs who have voluntarily left the parliament. The second regression model studies the correlation between the explanatory factors and which MPs left the parliament involuntarily over the years.

If we begin by studying which MPs have voluntarily left the parliament—the regression column on the left—it emerges that ambitious MPs are less likely than other MPs to choose to leave voluntarily. This means that the group of MPs who declared that they were no longer interested in remaining in the parliament—and where there was no underlying schism—is found primarily among MPs who *lack* career ambitions. The predicted probability of leaving the parliament voluntarily is 16 percentage points higher if an MP does not have career ambition (60 percent

Table 6.5 Reasons the MPs are no longer in the parliament for the 2006–2010 term (logit regression, odds ratio)

	Left the parliament voluntarily	Left the parliament involuntarily
Career ambition	.425*	1.757
Female	1.057	.869
Family background	1.206	1.442
Education	1.245	.350***
Age	.928**	.986
Professional politician	1.252	.577
Seniority	1.061**	.902**
Status	.197***	1.641
Political party		
Center Party	.166**	11.000***
Christian Democratic Party	.704	
Conservative Party	.263**	2.445
Green Party	.233	5.806***
Left Party	.990	3.320
Liberal Party	.567	1.955
Pseudo R^2	.189	.155
Number of persons	198	186

Sources: Parliamentary Study 1996; Mediearkivet; Presstext; Google; and Swedish Election Authority website.

Note: The first dependent variable ("Left the parliament voluntarily") is two-tailed. MPs who left the parliament voluntarily are coded as 1, and MPs who are still in the parliament for the 2006–2010 term or have left the parliament for other reasons are coded as 0. The second dependent variable ("Left the parliament involuntarily") is two-tailed. MPs who left the parliament involuntarily are coded as 1, and MPs who are still in the parliament for the 2006–2010 term or have left the parliament for other reasons are coded as 0. The independent variables are coded as follows: Career ambition: 0 = No career ambition, 1 = Career ambition; Female: 0 = Male, 1 = Female; Family background: 0 = Father blue-collar, 1 = Father small business owner or white-collar; Education: 0 = Not university educated, 1 = University educated; Occupation: 0 = Blue-collar, small business owner, and white-collar, 1 = Professional politician; Age: Serially according to age; Seniority: Serially by number of years in the parliament; Status: 0 = Have never held or have held a central party position, 1 = Have now a central party position. The Social Democratic Party is the reference category. *$p < .1$, **$p < .05$, ***$p < .001$. Robust standard errors.

versus 44 percent).[9] We can also see that MPs who lack status in the party organization are more likely to choose to leave voluntarily. The same applies to older and senior MPs.

Looking at the table's right column, we see that ambitious MPs have not been "forced" out of the parliament. Based on this aspect, we cannot say that career ambition obstructs the MPs' tenure in parliament. MPs without a university edu-

Table 6.6 Average scores in 1994 among MPs who left the parliament voluntarily

Career ambitions	
Yes	.08
No	.35

Sources: Parliamentary Study 1996; Mediearkivet; Presstext; Google; Swedish Election Authority website; Fakta om folkvalda 1998.
Note: The data are based on the MPs' career scores in 1994 and how the MPs left their seats in parliament. The higher the score, the more successful their career trajectory. The career score ranged from 0 to 5. All MPs who declared before the election that they did not want to remain in office and who did not report conflict or discontent as the reason were categorized as having left the parliament voluntarily.

cation are vulnerable, however, and at risk of having to leave the parliament involuntarily. Belonging to the Center Party and being a first-term MP also increase the risk. Ambitious MPs thus seem not to lose their enthusiasm after a time and leave: they do not give up voluntarily.

If we study which ambitious MPs have nevertheless left voluntarily, something interesting emerges. Those who left voluntarily were primarily the MPs who had low status in 1996. The MPs who left voluntarily in 1994 had an average career score of 0.08, which is far below the average for the parliament of 0.39. The career scores from 1994 are compared on Table 6.6 between MPs who voluntarily left the parliament based on their career ambitions.

The MPs who lack career ambitions and left the parliament voluntarily are in parity with the parliament average. Among the ambitious MPs, there is clear indication that those who have left the parliament are the less successful MPs. In other words, it is among ambitious MPs that career attainment has an effect, which may be contrasted with the ambitious MPs who left involuntarily. Their average score in 1994 was 1.1—almost three times higher than the average score. The main reason they fell out of the parliament was that their parties had lost seats.

These results correlate with the realistic expectations presented in the discussion of the definition of career ambition. We can see that there is a certain perspicacity among the MPs who choose to leave voluntarily. When success eludes them, they seem to rethink and step down.

MPS' CAREER STATUS IN 1994

This section will shed light on the MPs' actual careers, in particular whether ambitious MPs have experienced career success. We will begin the investigation

Table 6.7 MPs' career status in 1994 (OLS regression, beta standardized coefficients)

	MPs' status for the 1994–1998 term
Career ambition	.061
Female	.050
Family background	.095
Education	.010
Age	.079
Professional politician	.107
Seniority	.494***
Political party	
Center Party	.175*
Christian Democratic Party	.096
Conservative Party	.106
Green Party	.207*
Left Party	.071
Liberal Party	.096
Pseudo R^2	.280
Number of persons	204

Sources: Parliamentary Study 1996; Fakta om folkvalda 1998.
Note: The dependent variable consists of the MPs' career status in 1994. The scales goes from 0 to 5. The independent variables are coded as follows: Career ambition: 0 = No career ambition, 1 = Career ambition; Female: 0 = Male, 1 = Female; Family background: 0 = Father blue-collar, 1 = Father small business owner or white-collar; Education: 0 = Not university educated, 1 = University educated; Occupation: 0 = Blue-collar, small business owner, and white-collar, 1 = Professional politician; Age: Serially according to age; Seniority: Serially by number of years in the parliament. The Social Democratic Party is the reference category. *p < .1, **p < .05, ***p < .001. Robust standard errors.

by studying the MPs' status at the "starting line" in 1996.[10] In Chapter 3 I tested whether ambitious MPs were recruited for central party positions to a greater extent than other MPs. No systematic differences could be seen at that point. The analyses here, however, are broader and concern not only internal party conditions but also the MPs' status in the parliament.

When the MPs' average status score was compiled for 1996, it was 0.39.[11] Ambitious MPs had a somewhat higher average score, 0.54, but the difference is not significant, as shown in Table 6.7.

The results show that at the starting point for the study, ambitious MPs did not have an advantage. One thus cannot claim that ambitious MPs should be understood as the successful MPs in 1996. Even so, the results otherwise show that the longer an MP has served in the parliament, the greater the probability that he or she will obtain a high-status position. This may seem obvious, but it still matters to an extent, in that it indicates that the scoring system used is indeed effective.[12]

MPS' CAREER TRAJECTORY FROM 1996 TO 2006

The time has come to find out what actually happened in the ten years or so that elapsed since the MPs related their future plans. Have ambitious MPs had more successful careers than others?

The starting point for this investigation is that the MPs who were included in the 1996 study and were members of the parliament at the beginning of the 2006–2010 term are included in the calculation system. MPs who for various reasons are no longer in the parliament are assigned a score of zero, except for those who have left the parliament but hold a high-status position in the political system in 2006. This category includes the positions of county governor, director-general, and political office at the European level. In addition, MPs who have been a cabinet minister, speaker of the parliament, or party leader since 1994 but who left the parliament before 2006 are assigned points, based on the high status of these positions. Otherwise, the MPs' career status is calculated the same way as for the study of the MPs' career status in 1994. Table 6.8 shows that ambitious MPs differ significantly from their colleagues with respect to actual career attainments.

The main impression is that career attainment does not happen on its own. The table shows that career ambition does actually play a part in the MPs' success. Göran Persson's pronouncement that "He who wants to be chosen seldom is" does not appear to be true. The correlation between ambition and career attainment is also strengthened if you eliminate lower-status positions from the career calculation, such as assignments within the parliamentary group, which means that ambitious MPs have, above all, been successful at attaining the more prominent positions. MPs who had a high-status position in the party in 1996 have also experienced subsequent career success. And career attainment is more difficult for MPs from blue-collar homes. We can also confirm that women are as successful as men. If we go back to the numbers and look more specifically at the situation for ambitious men and women, however, there is a certain tendency that may indicate women are disadvantaged. More women with career ambitions (38 percent) have left the parliament voluntarily than men (19 percent). The gender differences among MPs who lack career ambitions are markedly smaller (men 57 percent and women 62 percent). If we examine the MPs' career trajectory from 1996 to 2006, ambitious men have gained an average increase of 0.40 points whereas ambitious women's scores increased by 0.13. This is thought-provoking, because the two groups had nearly equal scores in 1996. The average scores were 0.56 for men and

Table 6.8 MPs' career score in 2006 (OLS regression, standardized beta coefficients)

	MPs' career trajectory from 1996 to 2006
Career ambition	.145*
Female	−.014
Family background	.151**
Education	.063
Age	.246**
Professional politician	.097
Seniority	−.015
Status	.351**
Political party	
Center Party	−.039
Christian Democratic Party	−.092
Conservative Party	.042
Green Party	−.080
Left Party	.007
Liberal Party	.041
R^2	.287
Number of persons	201

Sources: Parliamentary Study 1996; Mediearkivet; Presstext; Google; Fakta om folkvalda 2010.

Note: The dependent variable consists of the career score that the MPs have acquired since 1996. The scale goes from 0 to 6. The independent variables are coded as follows: Career ambition: 0 = No career ambition, 1= Career ambition; Female: 0 = Male, 1 = Female; Family background: 0 = Father blue collar, 1 = Father small business owner or white-collar; Education: 0 = Not university educated, 1 = University educated; Occupation: 0 = Blue-collar, small business owner, and white-collar, 1 = Professional politician; Age: Serially according to age; Seniority: Serially by number of years in the parliament; Status: 0 = Have never held or have held a central party position, 1 = Have now a central party position. The Social Democratic Party is the reference category. *p < .1, **p < .05, ***p < .001. Robust standard errors.

0.5 for women. The sample is too small for me to draw any conclusions, but it may be an indicator that success does not come as easily for ambitious women MPs as it does for their male colleagues.

Based on the circumstance that ambitious MPs reported that they voted against their party more often than others, I have studied how beneficial such behavior is to their careers. This strategy proves to be a poor approach. MPs who report that they break with the party line more often than others have significantly worse career outcomes over time, as well as a lower average career score in 1994. MPs who want to achieve successful careers should therefore not rely solely on bucking the party leadership.

If we study the progress of MPs who reported that they often spoke at party group meetings, it proves that they achieved greater career attainment over time. They did not, however, have significantly higher status scores in 1996 when controlled for the same factors as on Table 6.8. The result is interesting because MPs who speak often at party group meetings are at risk of being perceived as attention-seekers. Considering how their careers have evolved over the years, loquacious individuals do not seem to be regarded as undesirable. It may be possible to connect this to the earlier discussions of the significance of cultivating a personal reputation and setting oneself apart. MPs who believe "silence is golden" may thus be wrong.

AMBITIOUS MPS SUCCEED

The MPs' personal career ambitions are a factor as we attempt to understand which politicians achieve the top positions in our representative democracy. There is a correlation between career ambition and career attainment. Ambition has a tangible effect primarily from the long-term perspective. The results show that ambitious MPs are younger than their colleagues when first elected to the parliament, but that the route from party membership to parliamentary debut is not faster. We have also been able to see that career ambitions have no effect on the MPs' capacity to gain a seat on their preferred committee. Nor are ambitious MPs better than others at retaining their seats in the parliament. They do, however, leave the parliament voluntarily to a lesser extent than other MPs, and those who leave are primarily those who have not been successful. Based on these results we can see that ambitious MPs do not suffer from their endeavors to achieve a political career. Ambition has either a positive effect or none at all. In that respect, career ambition is not a phenomenon that is penalized in the parliament. Those who strive to reach the top of the political hierarchy actually do well. One reason may be that the MPs we have followed in this book have a viable strategic approach. We can reconnect here to Donald Matthews's conclusions regarding American senators with ambitions to become presidents—those who simply followed the "Senate folkways" did not make it. Career attainment is not simply a matter of compliance: it also takes ambition and boldness to advance.

At the beginning of the chapter I recapped what we know so far about ambitious MPs. We can now augment that knowledge with the understanding that career ambition leads to career attainment. Ambitious MPs are a distinct group not only when it comes to socioeconomic status and how they behave in the parliament, but also with respect to their political careers. The results show that the drive to achieve career success makes a telling difference in a party-centric system like that in Sweden. When we therefore attempt to understand why we have the leading representatives we have, we cannot ignore that there in fact are politicians who have acted deliberately and strategically in order to one day attain a prominent position in our representative democracy and that they in fact succeed.

7. Is Sweden Different?

I contended in the introduction that Sweden may serve as an example of a political system where career ambition is not an effective motivator. What makes the case of Sweden interesting is that if career ambition is manifest in the parliament, there is good reason to assume that ambition is also an effective motivator in other parliamentary systems. We have now been able to confirm that there are MPs in the parliament who engage in long-term, committed, and goal-oriented career endeavors—and who achieve prominent political positions. In other words, the ambition to achieve career success makes a difference in a party-centric system like Sweden's. As the data have shown, 18 percent of the MPs in Sweden's parliament report an interest in a political career. In this chapter, I will take steps toward a comparative analysis with regard to the career ambitions of MPs in other European parliaments. The ambitions of Swedish parliamentarians will thus be put into an international context. The first question to be answered is whether 18 percent is a little or a lot from the European perspective.

The second general question is whether there are contextual factors that affect the proportion of ambitious MPs in the parliaments. In the event that variations exist among the parliaments, this will lead us to a discussion that relates to how institutional and cultural conditions affect the proportion of ambitious MPs. The chapter is accordingly split into two parts. In the first, we will study the Swedish case by putting it into a European context. The task of the second part will be to use the results uncovered in the first part to generate and then test hypotheses related to any similarities and differences between the parliaments.

MATERIAL

The international research project Political Representation in Europe (PRE) provides an opportunity to compare Swedish MPs with the parliamentarians of other countries. Between 1996 and 1997, surveys were sent to all national parliamentarians in eleven EU member states. The question asked of the Swedish MPs about their future plans was also put to their European colleagues. The eleven countries included in PRE are Belgium, France, Germany, Greece, Ireland, Italy, Luxembourg, Netherlands, Portugal, Spain, and Sweden. The response frequency for the study was 37.6 percent (N = 1,412). By international comparison, the Swedish political elite are exceptionally accommodating. Sweden had the highest response frequency in the PRE study, at 90 percent; Italy had the lowest, at 15 percent.[1] The level of representation is acceptable despite considerable variation in the distribution of responses.[2] Researchers from various parts of Europe have already studied the parliamentarians' PRE responses from several discrete perspectives, resulting in *The European Parliament, the National Parliaments, and European Integration* (Katz and Wessels 1999) and *Political Representation and Legitimacy in the European Union* (Schmitt and Thomassen 1999), as well as other publications. Thus far, however, no scholars have turned their attention to the parliamentarians' career ambitions.

PRE provides a unique opportunity to study the parliamentarians' ambitions, but the material nevertheless has limitations. One such limitation is the number of parliaments included in the study. While eleven Western European parliaments is not a poor sample, it is somewhat incomplete as a statistical basis for studying contextual explanations. Accordingly, some caution is called for with regard to interpretation of the results. Based on the material that exists, however, it is possible to make certain exploratory attempts.

POLITICAL AMBITION IN A EUROPEAN CONTEXT

Are there variations among the parliaments in the occurrence of ambitious MPs? Is the 18 percent found in the Swedish parliament a lot, a little, or somewhere in between? To answer these questions, I have used the same points of departure for the international comparison as in earlier chapters. The MPs who have indicated an interest in a position such as cabinet minister and/or positions within the EU organization are categorized as ambitious. The question on the international survey read, "What would you like to be ten years from now? Please tick as many as appropriate." Table 7.1 shows how the percentage of ambitious parliamentarians is distributed within each parliament. The parliament with the highest proportion of ambitious MPs is at the top of the table.

We can see that the proportion of ambitious MPs varies among the parliaments. Judging by Table 7.1, Sweden has relatively few ambitious MPs. Along with Luxembourg, the Netherlands, and Germany, Sweden is part of a group of "low-ambition countries." This group is followed by Belgium, France, Portugal, and Spain, where the proportion is between 41 and 48 percent. These countries are in turn followed by Italy and Ireland, which have a proportion of ambitious MPs of about 60 percent. The outlier is Greece: three-quarters of Greek parliamentarians report career ambition.

The sizable spread between the countries may indicate that there are institutional and/or cultural conditions that affect the proportion of ambitious MPs, but

Table 7.1 Proportion of ambitious MPs in the European parliaments

Country	Career ambitions (%)
Greece	75
Ireland	61
Italy	59
Spain	48
Portugal	48
France	45
Belgium	41
Netherlands	25
Germany	21
Sweden	18
Luxembourg	15
Number of persons	1,216

Source: Political Representation in Europe 1996.
Note: The question on the international survey was, "What would you like to be ten years from now? Please tick as many as appropriate." The MPs who have denoted interest in a position such as cabinet minister and/or positions within the EU organization are categorized as ambitious.

it may be wise to stop and think about whether the operationalization of career ambition might have something to do with these differences. Various positions in the EU organization, for example, are included among the political positions covered by the operationalization. One of the reasons for the large differences between the countries might be that support for the EU varies among the parliaments. As an example, one of the books that came out of the PRE project showed that Swedish MPs are less inclined to give up the reins of power to the EU than are other MPs, and that there are differences in the views of MPs in the various parliaments regarding how strong the EU as an institution should be in the future (Katz and Wessels 1999). This might be a contributing factor in the varying levels of interest from one parliament to the next in attaining positions within the EU organization. MPs from parliaments that are very enthusiastic about giving the EU more muscle might feel more enticed by the idea of going to Brussels than MPs from parliaments whose support is less wholehearted. This applies regardless of whether the positions per se have high status.

Table 7.2 shows the results of an analysis where the definition of career ambition was split into two: a broad definition that included both positions such as cabinet minister and positions within the EU organization, and a narrow definition that covered only the position in the national government.

Whether or not positions within the EU organization are included in the definition of career ambition has an impact on the analysis. The differences between

Table 7.2 Variation in the proportion of ambitious MPs depending upon the definition

Country	Broad career ambition (%)	Narrow career ambition (%)	Difference (%)
Greece	75	56	19
Ireland	61	47	14
Italy	59	33	26
Spain	48	25	23
Portugal	48	30	18
France	45	29	16
Belgium	41	29	12
Netherlands	25	12	13
Germany	21	17	4
Sweden	18	14	4
Luxembourg	15	5	10
Number of persons	1,216	1,216	

Source: Political Representation in Europe 1996.
Note: The question in the international survey was, "What would you like to be ten years from now? Please tick as many as appropriate." The MPs who denoted interest in the position of cabinet minister and positions within the EU organization belong to the category with broad career ambitions. The narrow definition includes only the position of cabinet minister. The difference was calculated by subtracting the narrow definition from the broad definition. See note 1 for the response frequencies for each country.

the countries are not as large when the narrower definition is used. The distance between the countries at either end of the spectrum, Greece and Luxembourg, declines by 9 percent, from 60 percent (75–15) to 51 (56–5). The average difference between the broad and narrow definitions is 14 percent. Sweden is still found in the category of "low-ambition countries" even when the narrow definition is used, and the same four countries still have the lowest proportion of ambitious MPs. We can thus confirm that the proportion of ambitious MPs varies among the parliaments. In this respect, political career ambition seems to be a motivator that is related to contextual factors.

Gordon Black, a scholar who has further developed Joseph Schlesinger's ambition theory (see Chapter 2), has posited that political institutions do not engender political ambition; instead, the structure of a political system acts as a filter that lets some candidates through while others are stopped (Black 1972). This implies that different political institutions provide ambitious MPs a different set of prerequisites for advancement. If we study the results shown in Table 7.2, it seems reasonable to assume that the political institutions cull ambitious MPs to varying degrees. Research in political science has shown in other contexts that how the institutions are structured affects both which candidates and which political parties are elected to the legislative assemblies (Duverger 1954; Gallagher 1991; Lijphart 1990; Norris 1996; Ordeshook and Shvetsova 1994; Taagepera and Shugart 1989).

Scholars who are preoccupied with, for example, the opportunities of women and ethnic minorities to participate in legislatures often study the design of electoral systems (for an overview, see Paxton, Hughes, and Painter 2010; Wängnerud 2009). In somewhat simplified terms, we might say that the less focus there is on the individual member, the more likely it becomes that individuals from underrepresented groups will be elected to legislatures (Kenworthy and Malami 1999; McAllister and Studlar 2002; Norris 1985; Paxton 1997; Reynolds 1999; Rule 1987).

Corruption researchers have also studied the significance of electoral systems and political representation. One much-debated result, for example, is that systems lacking any elements of direct election of individuals constrain voters' opportunities to demand accountability, and members are therefore more easily corruptible (see, e.g., Kunicová and Rose-Ackermann 2005; Persson, Tabellini, and Trebbi 2003).[3] In other words, researchers have studied the relationship between political institutions and life in parliament from various angles and found it fruitful.

In the following section, three possible causes of the variation in the proportion of ambitious MPs among the parliaments will be presented. The chapter concludes with a test of the hypotheses against one another in a multivariate regression, in which both the broad and narrow definitions are included.

FOCUS ON THE INDIVIDUAL

Researchers have previously drawn attention to the correlation between the structure of electoral systems and legislative members' incentives to market themselves. It has been shown that candidates work harder to cultivate a personal reputation in systems with distinct elements of preference voting than in systems that are less focused on the individual (Carey and Shugart 1995; Sartori 1976; Taagepera and Shugart 1989). Candidate-centered election makes it necessary for members to attract attention and thus become familiar to the electorate (Jacobson 2004). In Chapter 5 we were able to see that Swedish ambitious MPs were not averse to either standing out at party group meetings or breaking with the party line when voting in the chamber. We can therefore presume that ambitious MPs are people who want all eyes on them, and the greater scope a system provides for reputation-building, the more it benefits ambitious MPs. Likewise, we can imagine that systems that do not focus on individuals to any appreciable extent filter out ambitious politicians. The reason might be that when the parties themselves are able to decide which people will represent them, loyal team players are prized above individuals who cultivate a personal reputation. *Hypothesis 1 is therefore that electoral systems that include elements of preference voting favor ambitious MPs.*

ELECTION TURNOVER RATE FOR PARLIAMENTARIANS

Political ambition has to do with what the MPs intend to do in the future. The MPs' career ambitions may thus be affected by how many parliamentarians usually retain their seats after a general election. The turnover rate says something about the competition for seats in the parliament, as well as MPs' opportunities to plot out their long-term political futures (Matland and Studlar 2004).

There has been debate for some time in the United States concerning whether politicians retain their seats both far too long and far too comfortably (Herrick and Fisher 2007). Twenty-one states adopted term limits in the 1990s in the hope, among else, that higher turnover would result in the election of candidates of nonconventional background to state legislatures. The results were, however, not as anticipated. It is still the more affluent who enter politics (Carey et al. 2006). Researchers have been able to determine, however, that the legislators subjected to term limits modified their behavior. The members' relationships to their constituencies were weakened because the representatives expended less effort on keeping in touch with their constituents (ibid).

Nevertheless, the underlying idea of term limits is that the members' career plans are affected by how long they can possibly remain active within an institution. In such a case, this should indicate that ambitious MPs are affected by the turnover rate in their parliament. Low turnover in the parliament would imply that the MPs feel secure and thus have good opportunities to plan their future careers. But if many MPs in a parliament lose their seats at each election, this should have repercussions for the MPs' career ambitions, for the future is more uncertain. *Under hypothesis 2, a low turnover rate in connection with general elections stimulates the MPs' career ambitions.*

THE POLITICAL CULTURE

Table 7.1 showed us that there were large differences between the Southern European countries (plus Ireland) and the other countries. It might be possible to link one explanation for these differences to the political culture.[4] The significance of the political culture has been disputed over the years but has risen in estimation in the past decade (Fuchs 2007). Researchers who have studied women's political participation and conditions for being elected to parliament have pointed to the political culture as a significant factor (Wängnerud 2009). Among these scholars, some argue that the ideology prevailing within a party, or a country, has impact on which candidates are let through the filters (Caul 1999; Kenworthy and Malami 1999; Kittilson 2006; Kunovich and Paxton 2005; Lovenduski and Norris 1993). Beliefs about what distinguishes a good politician also reflect who become parliamentarians (Eagly, Makhijani, and Klonsky 1992; Lawless and Theriault 2005).

Sweden is one of the most gender-equal countries in the world (Atkinson, Rainwater, and Smeeding 1995). If quotations from Swedish politicians are reliable, the country's citizenry also exhibit a sort of "tall poppy syndrome"—the tendency to criticize more affluent or more successful people. In its own way, this tall poppy syndrome could be a manifestation of the greater difficulty ambitious politicians have in asserting themselves in an egalitarian society. We have certainly been able to see that ambitious MPs nonetheless do well in the Swedish parliament. They achieve success not due to the Swedish political culture, but in spite of it.

It is not easy to test the degree of equality, but I will make the attempt. I have already pointed out that there are researchers who argue that the proportion of women in a parliament is an expression of a society's egalitarian values (see, e.g., Graubard 1986; Ingelhart and Norris 2003; Liebig 2000; Norris 1996). Quite simply, it is easier for women to participate in the legislative assemblies of more gender-equal societies. Accordingly, how I measure the degree of egalitarian values in the political system is based on what proportion of the members of parliament are women. I have also created an alternative measure of gender equality, based on Gini coefficients, which are commonly used to measure inequality of income in a country (see, e.g., Deininger and Squire 1996; Jordahl 2009; Persson and Tabellini 1994). I use Gini coefficients as a method of testing whether the proportion of women in parliament is a reliable measure of gender equality. If we reconnect the gender equality argument to the first chapter of the book and to people's innate dislike of people who seem power hungry, this dislike should quite simply be more intense in societies that promote the principle of gender equality. *Hypothesis 3 is thus that political environments more oriented toward gender equality will affect the MPs' career ambitions.*

THE EFFECTS OF INSTITUTIONAL AND CULTURAL FACTORS ON MPS' CAREER AMBITIONS

In the final regression table of the book, I analyze which factors have a correlation with parliamentarians' ambitions. The three hypotheses will be tested and com-

Table 7.3 Effects of three factors on MPs' career ambitions (logit regression, odds ratio)

	Broad career ambition	Narrow career ambition
Contextual factors		
Focus on the individual	.159	.092
Opportunities for the MPs to plan their futures over time	–.000	.038**
The political culture	–.058**	–.032**
Sociopolitical factors		
Female	–.167	.038
Education	.615***	.730**
Professional politician	.229	.241
Age	–.407**	–.292*
Seniority	–.008	–.086
Ideology	.076	.138***
Pseudo R^2	.101	.090
Number of persons	1,130	1,130

Sources: Political Representation in Europe 1996. For information about preference voting, see LeDuc, Niemi, and Norris 1996. The data on the turnover rate in the parliament were taken from Lijphart 1999. The turnover rate is calculated as an average value from a number of elections retrospectively. The data on the proportion of women in the parliaments was taken from Inter-Parliamentary Union statistics, available on the organization's website: http://www.ipu.org/wmn-e/classif-arc.htm.

Note: The question in the international survey was, "What would you like to be ten years from now? Please tick as many as appropriate." The MPs who denoted interest in the position of cabinet minister and positions within the EU organization belong to the category with broad career ambitions. The narrow definition includes only the position of cabinet minister. The dependent variable is two-tailed (0–1). The results in the table are controlled for gender, age (three-tailed), seniority (three-tailed), education (not university educated, university educated), political ideology (respondents placed themselves on a left–right scale from 0 to 10), occupational background 0–1 (other occupational categories, professional politician). The contextual variables are coded as follows: Preference voting: 0 = No, 1 = Yes. The proportion of MPs who retain their seats after an election is a continuous variable between 54.8 and –78.7. The proportion of women in the parliament is a continuous variable between 6.3 and 42.7. All countries are weighted equally, and the standard errors are clustered at the country level. $*p < .1$, $**p < .05$, $***p < .001$.

pared to each other. The regression model also includes in the individual factors: gender, education, age, occupational background, tenure in the parliament, and ideological self-assessment on the left-right scale. My intent is to use the same control variables as in Chapter 4, but because it is not possible to collect data on recruitment, language skills, status, and so on, these variables are not included. Instead of party size and left-wing/right-wing bloc, I use the MPs' self-placement on the left-right scale, as Swedish conditions are difficult to translate to the European context.

Table 7.3 shows that there is a correlation between political culture and the MPs' career ambitions. The most stable measure is of the degree of egalitarianism in the society. The results are significant regardless of whether the definition of career ambition is broad or narrow. The stability remains even when the material is tested against other independent variables, such as the occurrence of minority governments, governmental power, and constituency size. The results are also robust when the other measure, Gini coefficient, of equality is used. In the various tests performed on the material, there are bivariate differences between men and women with regard to career ambition, but the differences are eliminated in multivariate regression analyses. Women MPs are per se not the explanation for why there is a correlation between the proportion of women in a parliament and ambitious politicians. The correlation seems instead to be related to the context itself. In settings where it is easier for women to assert themselves, there are also fewer ambitious MPs. My conclusion is that there is a relationship between equality and ambition.

As only eleven countries are included in the study, the results are relatively "sensitive." If, for instance, we study the two institutional factors of preference voting and turnover rate, both factors are highly dependent upon which other background factors are used. They are not robust in the same manner as the measures of political culture. The regression table nevertheless shows that preference voting has no effect, but there are indications that turnover rate might have an effect on the MPs' career ambitions. This applies only, however, provided that the ambitions refer to the national government—the narrow definition, that is—which may be logical in and of itself. The MPs who are primarily aiming for career attainment at home are more dependent on the turnover rate in their own parliament. MPs who would also like to achieve success in the EU are not as dependent upon national conditions.

If we study which individual explanatory factors are important, it emerges that well-educated people who lean toward the right are more interested in a political career. In the Swedish case, these factors were not as central. That education has an impact in the international survey, but not the Swedish one, may have a simple explanation. The international survey did not include any information about the MPs' family backgrounds. If we redo the Swedish analysis but omit the parents' occupational backgrounds from the regression model, education also becomes significant in Sweden. This suggests that education indicates a class perspective in the international survey as well. It is harder to explain why MPs who place themselves to the right on the left-right scale are more interested in a political career. The left-right scale has no effect whatsoever in the Swedish material. In Chapter 4 we were able to determine that only the Green Party differed. But on the international stage, there seem to be ideological differences in relation to the MPs' career ambitions.

In contrast to the Swedish case, professional politicians are not more ambitious in an international comparison, but I say this with some reservations. The data on the MPs' occupational backgrounds was collected by asking the MPs on the survey itself what their occupation was before they were elected to the parliament. There is a tendency, at least in the Swedish case, for MPs to not tick the "professional politician" box. When the MPs who participated in the 1996 Swedish Parliamentary Study self-reported their occupational backgrounds, only slightly above 5 percent were what we refer to as professional politicians. But if we use register data, it emerges that nearly 37 percent of the MPs were in fact professional politicians when they were elected to the parliament. Consequently, I suspect that the importance of being a professional politician is underestimated in Table 7.3. Otherwise, we can note that how we define career ambition does not make much of a difference. The results are relatively robust regardless of whether the definition is broad or narrow.

SWEDEN AND POLITICAL CAREER AMBITION

This chapter has shown that the claims to generalizability that I made early in the book are accurate. From an international perspective, there are few MPs in the Swedish parliament with political career ambitions. As ambitious MPs make a distinct impression in the Swedish context, there is good reason to assume that the same also applies in other parliaments.

Based on the exploratory attempts to explain the differences among the parliaments, a correlation is found between career ambition and egalitarianism. The proportion of ambitious MPs is connected to the level of equality in a society. This is interesting because the results confirm the assertion that there is a "tall poppy syndrome" in Sweden that affects our politicians. Equality may therefore be involved and influence which motivators are manifested in a parliament. Based on these results, we can consider how the parliaments are affected by the proportion of ambitious MPs. Does it make any difference if 18 percent or 75 percent of MPs are politically ambitious? Unfortunately, the available material does not allow me to answer that question in any meaningful way.

We do know that ambitious MPs are not a negligible force in the legislative assemblies and that there seem to be significant differences between the parliaments that can be traced back to political culture. If we follow the direction of this tangent, it indicates that this may also reflect the field of candidates. When the American experimental scholars presented in Chapter 1 encouraged action to influence public trust in the political system, it was by creating the perception that politicians become powerful "without making any conscious effort to do so" (Smith et al. 2007:269). That exhortation may be difficult to heed in political systems whose main field consists of ambitious MPs who are prepared to fight hard in the competition for the foremost positions in the representative democracy.

8. Ambition in Representative Democracy

Competition for political office is critical to the function of a democratic system. A representative democracy without political representatives who compete for power is unthinkable. Nevertheless, the personal motivations of individual representatives for seeking power are a controversial subject. On the European horizon, there has been emphasis on the principle that the political parties should curry the favor of the electorate and not the individuals who represent the parties. For this reason, the study of political ambition has been neglected for too long. Political memoirs and research in this field have communicated the idea that the personal motivations of representatives do not further our understanding of the workings of our democratic systems.

The point of departure has been the opposite in the American context. American scholars have instead presumed that representatives are motivated by personal gain and have designed their studies—and their political system—accordingly. Politicians' ambitions to hold high offices are one of the premises of the American national structure. One of the Founding Fathers, James Madison, articulated the matter thus:

> Ambition must be made to counteract ambition. The interest of the man must be connected with the constitutional rights of the place. It may be a reflection on human nature, that such devices should be necessary to control the abuses of government. But what is government itself, but the greatest of all reflections on human nature? If men were angels, no government would be necessary. If angels were to govern men, neither external nor internal controls on government would be necessary. (Madison, *The Federalist Papers* no. 51, 1788)

Madison expressed the distinct notion that we can never ignore the ambitions of the powerful. He also presumed that ambition is a component of our nature, and thus to be ambitious is to be human. Ambitious politicians are a reality that must be controlled. But that which is seen as something "human" from an American perspective might instead be something that is "system dependent." In this book, I have viewed both the European and the American perspectives on political ambition in a critical light. It is difficult to talk about human motivations, as the Americans do, if these motivations are not manifest in political systems that are structured otherwise. It is conceivable that the personal ambitions of politicians may have been constrained in systems with strong parties that have distinct collective values.

This final chapter is intended to provide an overview of the empirical and methodological analyses as well as to consider the implications of my results on how we should think about the role of political ambition in representative democracy. I will also take the liberty of pointing ahead to future studies of political ambition.

EMPIRICAL CONCLUSIONS

The main message of this book is that ambitious MPs are found in many different types of political settings. Even in the Swedish context, where they are said not to exist, they are both active and successful. My analyses show that almost one-fifth of the MPs in the Swedish parliament in 1996 made up the theoretical basis upon which we can speak of politicians with real career ambitions.

Who are they then, these ambitious ones? The book has clarified that ambitious MPs are not randomly distributed among parliamentarians. They are often younger individuals from relatively affluent families, residents of the Stockholm area, and professional politicians when first elected to the parliament. We have also seen that ambitious MPs, based on the arguments in the theoretical literature on various representation styles, may be likened to Burkeans (Eulau et al. 1959). The individual voter and the constituency are less important to them. They instead emphasize the importance of their personal convictions and of making their voices heard in various contexts, such as by breaking with the party line. The ambitious are also more engaged in international issues and more likely to see themselves as internationalists. When it comes to internal party machinations, ambitious MPs put more emphasis on playing the inside game than do other MPs. The inside game includes cultivating good relationships with the party leadership, standing up to party opinion, and winning debates at party group meetings. The MPs can therefore be said to have a distinct strategic approach to their work in the parliament and in the parliamentary party group.

It is interesting to note that in none of the analyses undertaken in Chapter 6 did it emerge that ambitious MPs are disadvantaged when it comes to committee assignments or other career positions. I found no support for the notion that ambition constrains the individual MP. On the contrary, ambitious MPs have been more successful than others over time. The results are reinforced by eliminating lower-status positions, such as member of the parliamentary group, from the analysis. Ambitious Swedish MPs are thus not passed over when leading positions are filled.

The European comparison showed that there are relatively few ambitious MPs in the Swedish parliament compared to other Western European parliaments. The proportion of Swedish ambitious MPs is the second-lowest in a European comparison. I also established that there are large variations among the parliaments with regard to how many of their seats are filled with ambitious MPs. The conditions and prerequisites for those aspiring to career attainment probably differ from one parliament to the next. Nonetheless, the results indicate that the low proportion of Swedish ambitious MPs can be related to a culture of equality that constrains the field of ambitious MPs. We might speculate as to whether the difficulty Southern European parliamentarians have in arriving at a consensus on things like how to manage economic crises is related to their supply of politicians. When Sweden was affected by similar problems in the early 1990s, the country was able in a spirit of parliamentary unity to bolster the country's finances and create financial regulations that are still respected by the parties. It may be more difficult for legislatures that harbor a large proportion of ambitious MPs to manage large structural problems because the MPs do not feel they can afford to upset their voters and thus choose to avoid the tough decisions in favor of the easy ones.

Alan Ehrenhalt (1991) concluded in his book about American politics that what has changed the most over the years in Congress is ambition. The system is, more than ever, open for political careers. Though Ehrenhalt's book is somewhat dated, his conclusions remain relevant. According to Ehrenhalt there are no longer any barriers in terms of a party elite for politicians with career ambitions. The only things that hold candidates back are all the time and all the money they need to spend on a political career. These are strong selectors, though. The only individuals who make it to Congress are those who are very ambitious to hold office. At the same time, the US political culture has changed, with values such as equality, individualism, and openness becoming increasingly important (ibid). When these ingredients are combined with ambition, the effectiveness of a political system is in danger: "Our political system, top to bottom, needs leadership, discipline, and the willingness of individuals to submerge their personal preferences for the common good. When the system fails consistently to provide these qualities, generating a politics of posturing and stalemate, we conclude that the people we elected have let us down" (ibid., 275).

Looking at the Congress of today, Ehrenhalt's pessimistic prediction is quite accurate. Madison's idea that one man's ambition must be balanced by others men's (and women's) ambition is perhaps not enough. When ambition is counteracted, it is hard to get anything done. Maybe ambition must not only be countered but also be complemented with collectivistic ideas about the common good.

It could be worth mentioning that encouraging the capability to decide and realizing the will of the people are so pertinent in the United States that the American Political Science Association created a "task force" whose objective was to create ideas for more efficient decision-making procedures. The members of the task force identified the capacity to act as a core democratic quality (Warren and Mansbridge 2013). We should not forget the value of *acting* in the interest of the people in a manner responsive to them (Pitkin 1967).

EMPIRICAL IMPLICATIONS

The main inspiration for the study of which MPs have career ambitions was found in sociological advances. Looking at the MPs' socioeconomic status was a fruitful way to predict which politicians aspire to attain the top positions in a representative democracy. The ambition to achieve career success is relatively clearly linked with politicians who were already professional politicians when first elected to the parliament.

Today, the position as elected representative at the elite level is a paid occupation. When the Swedish diet of the four estates was transformed in 1867 to a bicameral parliament, only the members of the lower house were paid. After World War II, reforms were implemented that paved the way for the professionalization of politics. Wages increased, the parliamentary session was extended, and a pension system was introduced. During the 1970s the Swedish parliament became a workplace populated by full-time paid politicians and civil servants. The base salary for MPs in 2016 was SEK 62,400 per month; the average pay of a state employee was just over SEK 31,600 the same year (Statistics Sweden pay data-base). MPs may apply for up to SEK 50,000 per term in travel grants for fact-finding trips. MPs who live more than 50 km from the house of parliament have the right to a short-stay residence. They are entitled to a maximum rent subsidy of SEK 8,600 or the free use of one of the 250 short-stay apartments provided by the parliament (information taken from the Riksdag's website). Moreover, public acceptance has been established for the principle that the political system should provide political "retirement" positions—such as being appointed as an ambassador, county governor, director-general, or various types of board service (see, e.g., Fichtelius 2007; Isaksson 2002). Politics has become a way of life. Former Social Democratic minister of foreign affairs Lennart Bodström wrote in his memoirs that some of the difficulties he encountered in politics were related to entering the political arena at a relatively late age (fifty-four). Bodström believes one must be aware of the problems that can arise upon entering high-level politics as a neophyte (Bod-ström 2000). If the trend continues and the parliament gains increasing numbers of professional politicians, it might lead to an increase in the proportion of ambi-tious MPs, which may have consequences for who will have a chance at attaining the top political positions in the future. Meanwhile, there is another tendency that may result in the opposite situation—fewer ambitious MPs. Swedish MPs are sit-ting for increasingly shorter periods in the parliament (Ahlbäck Öberg, Hermans-son, and Wängnerud 2007). What impact will this trend have on MPs' interest in working long-term to build a career? As the MP turnover rate increases, long-term career endeavors may be affected. If fewer people want to invest in a political ca-reer, the parties will have to manage MPs who want to make a splash but are less in-terested in staying on and doing the unglamorous day-to-day work. A parliament made up of a large proportion of first-termers may lead to weakened vigilance over the governing administration and to giving the executive branch too much latitude (Kurtz, Cain, and Niemi 2007). Legislatures with high turnover rates are at risk, in other words, of losing valuable competence if the members come and go (Cain and Kousser 2004; Kousser 2006; Maestas 2000). Likewise, we need representatives who are willing to stay in their seats, in part so that the electorate can hold them accountable (Aars 1997).

Given that it is primarily professional politicians who strive to achieve the prominent positions and that the people who are currently active in politics have been recruited within narrow frameworks, there is reason to consider the poten-tial consequences. More than half of newly elected municipal representatives in Sweden have someone in their immediate circle who already holds or has held elected office (Nielsen 2001). International studies provide evidence that young people who want to run for office have been socialized by politically active parents (Cross and Young 2008). One might dramatize this course of events by saying that political representation is on the way to becoming a family affair. For this reason, it would be problematic if the ambition to attain the highest positions in Sweden's representative democracy were reserved to those who already have connections in the party machine (Dal Bó, Dal Bó, and Snyder 2009).

In order to broaden the parties' recruitment base, the ambition to achieve a successful career in politics should reach beyond the political class. Greater aware-ness of the value of political ambition could also contribute to the internal revi-talization of the parties. If the candidates who are interested in a position openly declare their commitment and state why they want that particular office, it could pave the way to vitalization. If, in connection with this, party members are offered the opportunity by means of preference voting to choose who will represent them in various matters, we might leave behind the relatively small circles that currently nominate the party representatives. A more open procedure for the appointment of various representative positions would also make it easier for potential candidates who have only been party members for a short time to gain legitimacy, as they would have been elected by party members.

We should not, however, ignore the possible risks of encouraging MPs' personal career ambitions. One question, for example, is what other forces the parties would unleash if candidates were allowed to compete for political positions with no further ado. As we already know, internal nomination processes do not bring out the best in people (see, e.g., Kirkpatrick 1976; Roback 1975; Southwell 1986). Heightened focus on individual candidates who fight it out in public might not have any ameliorating effect. Open candidacies might also make it more difficult to overcome internal antagonisms once the dust has settled. In the event of numerous challengers to the party leadership, the party may find it difficult to advance as a strong collective actor.

It has also emerged in this study that ambitious MPs are not penalized by their colleagues. This dichotomy is an undeniably interesting subject for further exploration. On the one hand, leading politicians claim that those who want to be chosen seldom are. On the other hand, ambitious MPs are successful MPs. One might well ask whether ambitious MPs play their cards so close to their chests that no one around them realizes they harbor career ambitions, or whether there is—despite all—an acceptance of ambition among MPs. Considering that ambitious MPs are inclined to cultivate a personal reputation, it seems unlikely that the answer would be that they have managed to fly below the radar. On the contrary: these MPs work to attract attention, and their colleagues in the parliament must obviously like what they see. If this were not so, ambitious MPs would have had no chance. This provides reason to more closely study how ambitious MPs behave when the leading positions at the party's disposal are allocated. In the process of collecting the data on the MPs' careers, I have also thought about why certain MPs who have sat in the parliament for several terms have not attained any positions beyond a standing seat on a committee. Success is, despite all, one reason MPs want to remain in office (Ahlbäck Öberg, Hermansson, and Wängnerud 2007; Moore and Hibbing 1992). What drives them to continue their political pursuits? Should we regard these MPs as loyal team players who do not ask much for themselves, or as people who abstain from conflicts and debates in order to achieve a comfortable life in parliament, all things considered?

One of the most interesting implications of the European comparison has to do with the political culture and its relationship to career ambition. I would like to particularly stress the correlation between egalitarian societies and ambitious MPs. In other contexts, researchers have found that there is a relationship between equality and social trust (Newton 2007). In egalitarian societies, people put more trust in each other (Putnam 1993; Seligman 1997). Studies also show that inequality is what affects the degree of trust (Rothstein and Uslaner 2005). Inequality also affects how much citizens trust politicians (Schäfer 2010). The correlation between social inequality, civic trust in elected representatives, and the proportion of ambitious MPs is thus thought-provoking. Experimental studies have shown that citizens actually dislike a political system if they believe the system is populated by the ambitious. For this reason, the researchers recommended that steps be taken to make it so that people believe officials have been elected to office for reasons other than their efforts to that end (Smith et al. 2007). Political trust is high in Sweden; from an international perspective, Swedish citizens live in an egalitarian society and there are relatively few ambitious MPs in the political system. Based upon these research findings, we might say that what we are seeing when Swedish politicians play down and deny the importance of career ambition is the manifestation of the "wisdom of crowds." This deemphasis perhaps helps prevent public perceptions of politicians as self-interested actors and thus contributes to greater trust in the political system.

Nonetheless, it is conceivable that the restrictive attitude comes at a price. People who are willing to challenge the entrenched powers in the parties are essential; in so doing, they subject the people in power to competition, and competition is beneficial to intraparty dynamics (Pareto 1935) and the country as a whole (Besley, Persson, and Sturm 2010). We need candidates with the courage to challenge the status quo and do this so deftly that they avoid penalties. Still, unreservedly removing restraints on ambition is probably untenable.

METHODOLOGICAL CONCLUSIONS

The general methodological conclusion of the book is simple: political ambition can be studied using the same methods applied to other political phenomena. Ambition is certainly a delicate subject and a complex phenomenon, but asking a straightforward question about what MPs want to be doing in ten years can identify it.

When I began to study the subject, I turned to the classical philosophers for help in determining what requirements could reasonably be imposed to identify a person as ambitious. The philosophers' reasoning focused my search on people who demonstrated long-term commitment, goal-orientation, and willingness to act in order to attain difficult objects. To these criteria, I added the American approach to studying political ambition—advancement from one institution to another. In that the survey question encompassed characteristics that, for example, required the MPs to decide whether they were interested in positions that were not immediate prospects and that meant that the MP would have to move to another institution, the survey material fulfilled the initial necessary requirements for validity. In the next validity test, it emerged that the MPs had understood that the political positions did not lie in their immediate futures. In the same way, the MPs' interest in prominent positions did not fade depending on the duration of their tenure in the parliament. As such, it is an interesting and to some extent contrasting result in relation to Gaddie's findings. In his book about political careers Gaddie concluded that "Ambitions are not always fully conceptualized when a politician seeks office and that personal and political events will shape ambition through the career and the life cycle" (2004:199).

According to Gaddie's findings there is an ongoing interaction between the politician and the institutional possibilities in front of him or her. Ambitious MPs do have staying power, which was clearly manifested when they were compared as a group to MPs interested in a career in the parliament, or in the words of Herrick and Moore (1993)—intrainstitutional ambitions. After serving just one term, only a tiny fraction of MPs report that they have intrainstitutional ambitions. There seems to be something about the political events and the MPs that makes MPs reevaluate their ambition to make a career within the parliament. From that perspective, intrainstitutional ambitions are more related to the expectations the newcomers have when they enter the parliament and what they experience in the parliament. Intrainstitutional ambitions fade away after just one term in the parliament, whereas politicians with progressive ambitions are more committed to their goals. That is important for our understanding of progressive ambitions. Politicians with career ambitions have true ambitions and aim high—and these aims are not related to the immediate opportunities in front of them. A politician who seizes the moment might be better characterized as an opportunist. An opportunist reacts to current events and evaluates his or her chances based on that. If this is a correct interpretation, it makes sense that MPs with intrainstitutional ambitions do not behave in a distinctive way and that politicians with career ambitions play the long game.

Moreover, there is a link between MPs who say they would like to have a position and those MPs' behavior. That link is central to our understanding of political career ambition. If no such pattern had been revealed, it would have been difficult to conclude that we were dealing with ambitious MPs. Instead, we would have been compelled to find that while there are certainly MPs who would like to have more prominent positions, their hopes and wishes are on the whole just that and nothing more. This kind of MP would be more in-line with the politicians Gaddie discussed in his book. One difference between the studies, though, is that in the Swedish case we are dealing with the absolute political elite. A step below, politicians might be less assure where they would like to take their political career and are therefore more sensitive to the ebb and flood tides of the political cycle.

The large difference between MPs interested only in a career in the parliament and ambitious MPs is key in validating the survey question. It shows that the ambition to move to another institution is essential to the understanding of ambitious MPs. This in turn strengthens my conviction that including not only the distinctions made by the classical philosophers but also the established American research was the right thing to do in the study of career ambition in European parliaments.

METHODOLOGICAL IMPLICATIONS

I have been able to show that the MPs' career ambitions can be studied based on simple survey questions. It may be that the strength of the questions about future plans resides in their very simplicity. If I had set about constructing questions about MPs' career ambitions, I would surely have asked them to report how much they wanted a particular position, how they assessed their chances of obtaining it, and what it would take for them to succeed. If the questions were of that nature, the MPs would have had to more overtly "admit" that they harbor personal career ambitions, which might not have been to the advantage of the study. The relatively restrained survey question that I used meant that the MPs were not forced to confront their own ambitions as openly, which may have made the whole thing easier.[1]

Because the adopted definition emphasizes that to be considered ambitious, politicians must have a long-term commitment to attaining their objects, politicians who aspire to a position "here and now" drop out, which may come at a price. Life in politics can be a roller-coaster. People who have never considered participating in the larger contexts, or for that matter have never been considered for such positions, are suddenly presented with an opportunity to rapidly climb the career ladder. Within the space of a couple of weeks, they begin to position themselves as viable candidates for a particular position. The question is, can such a person rightly be categorized *as an ambitious politician*? According to the definition established here, the answer would be no. Key ingredients like long-term commitment and goal-orientation are missing. Nonetheless, such a politician aspires to a more prominent position. In these cases, following Gaddie's claim, we might perhaps speak of politicians with *short-term* career ambitions. It emerged in Chapter 5 that the behavior of professional politicians in general was consistent with the picture of ambitious MPs—that they must kowtow to the party leadership and tone down their personal reputation. Researchers engaged in future studies should perhaps keep this in mind and design a question that makes it possible to differentiate between MPs with long-term versus short-term career ambitions.

The current definition of career ambition can be used to develop the arguments surrounding the desire for advancement. In one category, we have ambitious MPs; those who both want a particular object and act to attain it. In the other category we find MPs who want a particular object but are making no active attempt to improve their prospects. In addition to these, there is a set of MPs who would not want a prominent position even if they were recruited. Our understanding of career ambition could be elaborated if we deepened our knowledge about the difference between those who strive for career attainment and those who are simply not interested.

The definition I have devised is closely tied to ambitious MPs in the parliament. In the event that one wanted to study the significance of ambition in local politics, for example, or political youth organizations, or among the public at large, there would be reason to ponder how the phenomenon can best be identified. It would be interesting in the context to follow active members of the youth organizations in a longitudinal study and study how their career ambitions evolve over time. In this context, we could also gain an understanding of how the interplay between socioeconomic resources, encouragement, and early success affects an individual's willingness to invest in a political career. We would thus learn something more about the people who will one day reach the heights of the political hierarchy and govern the country.

FUTURE RESEARCH ON POLITICAL CAREER AMBITION

This book provides a clear reference for future research regarding the study of the personal motivations of individual politicians. The results that emerged in the book provide favorable prerequisites for proceeding with the study of political career ambition. I have been able to show that ambition has impact as both a dependent and independent variable. In short, ambitious politicians are a factor to consider when we are aiming to understand what is happening in representative democracy.

However, many challenges remain. Researchers have once again begun aiming their spotlights at the personalities of politicians and how personality influences political engagement. There may be countless reasons behind the engagement. James Payne and Oliver Woshinsky (1972:519) argued that motivations like "I want to do what's best for the country" and "I got into politics to prevent water pollution" are far too intellectualized to suffice as explanations for why people become full-time politicians. They posited that other factors must be considered in order to understand why politicians choose to skip meals, give up spending time with the family, and suffer sleepless nights in order to attain their ends. For these researchers, one such factor is that politicians are driven by emotions that must be satisfied. These involve feeling important, gaining status, and performing something meaningful for future generations (ibid., 519ff).

Based on this reasoning, representative democracy cannot be detached from the inner lives of elected representatives. According to Ronald Reagan, it was his previous success that made him want to see how far his wings could carry him: "I never in my wildest dreams ever aspired to public service. I loved that world that I was in, the entertainment world. So, the very fact that I'd been blessed with some success and could attract an audience, I thought that it was only right that I should use that in behalf of causes that I believed in. So, I don't know what I could have done differently" (quoted in Barber 1985:489–490). Reagan thus pointed out that talent, inclination, and success were what made him fight for what he believed in.

When Richard Nixon agreed to be interviewed by David Frost in 1977, the conversation turned to what is meaningful in life. Nixon said that people who believe that life would be perfect if only they were millionaires and living the life of Reilly are wrong. Such a life, Nixon continued, lacked something essential. "What makes life mean something is purpose. A goal. The battle. The struggle. Even if you don't win it." Life must, according to Nixon, have a greater purpose, and to achieve it, one must be willing to do battle. The ambition to reach the highest echelons of representative democracy may thus contribute to making the day-to-day life of politics meaningful to the MP who struggles with discontented voters and critical journalists. The motivation to achieve career success can also be reduced to the possession of power per se. Senator John McCain wrote openly about his reasons for running in the Republican presidential primary in 2000: "I didn't decide to run for president to start a national crusade for the political reforms I believed in or to run a campaign as if it were some grand act of patriotism. In truth, I wanted to be president because it had become my ambition to be president. . . . In truth, I'd had the ambition for a long time" (McCain and Salter 2002:373).

Researchers are also becoming more aware that individuals' psychological dispositions influence how they form their understanding of politics or act in political contexts (Mondak 2010). One of the most interesting fields of political science research at the moment is research on the "Big Five" (Ozer and Benet-Martinez 2006). According to this research tradition, the Big Five are a number of dimensions that have to do with whether a person is open to experience, conscientious, extraverted, agreeable, and emotionally stable (McCrae and Costa 1999). An individual's openness to experience has, for example, been shown to have a link to their political views (Van Hiel, Kossowska, and Mervielde 2000). This research previously focused on people in general but recently has examined people within the political elite (Caprara et al. 2003). There is much that remains to be done in this respect and thus tremendous scope for comparative studies. There is a general focus on the quality of institutions, but less on the quality of the people who will populate them. One problem with changing a political system may have to do with the field of available politicians. If chiefly one type of politician runs for office or wins elections, the revitalization that might be sorely needed may never occur. For this reason, I would like to end by quoting V. O. Key, who pithily expresses my main conclusion: "The nature of the workings of government depends ultimately on the men who run it. The men we elect to office and the circumstances we create that affect their work determine the nature of popular government. Let there be emphasis on those we elect to office" (Key 1956:10).

Key is right. We absolutely should study the individuals who are fighting to attain the highest positions in our democratic system.

NOTES

1. Cherie Maestas underscores the central role of career ambition in the American understanding of politics as follows: "The idea that ambition for office shapes the behavior of political leaders is hardly new, nor is it often disputed" (Maestas 2003: 440).

2. There is evidence, however, that women who are believed to be power-hungry are judged more harshly by others (Okimoto and Brescoll 2010).

3. In *Guns, Germs, and Steel* (1997) professor of physiology Jared Diamond argues that environmental and technical differences caused people to form larger societies and abandon small, egalitarian tribes.

4. Niccolo Machiavelli's analysis is perhaps the clearest example of why people mistrust individuals seeking a political career. *The Prince* gives us a glimpse into a crass reality in which politicians act beyond ethical considerations in the pursuit of power and riches. In the world depicted by Machiavelli, necessity must be made a virtue (rather than to act virtuously by necessity). The rulers are playing a dirty game, whose end is survival. This is not, however, something a ruler should publicly reveal; instead, a prince must *appear* exemplary. A prince should "appear merciful, faithful, humane, religious, [and] upright". When, however, the situation so demands, the prince must change his shape: "but the mind should remain so balanced that were it needful not to be so, you should be able and know how to change to the contrary" (Machiavelli 2001 chapter 18:6). If circumstances change, the ruler's characteristics should also change. Machiavelli's advice to those who aspired to the throne was to be as cunning as a fox when snares have been laid and as terrifying as a lion when his enemies are poised to attack. The problem for most rulers, according to Machiavelli, is that they were often either one or the other, but not both. In his studies of elites, Vilfredo Pareto elaborated on Machiavelli's classification and pointed out that there are different types of elites who exercise their power in different ways. There are those who force others into submission (lions), and those who take control over material resources and by that means induce people to bend to their wishes (foxes). According to Pareto, foxes and lions come into conflict with one another, and the lions vanquish the foxes. But after some time on the throne, lions are transformed into foxes and thus lose power. In this way, new elites rise to challenge the old (Pareto 1935).

5. Thomas Hobbes reasoned differently. To him, the results a leader could deliver were the only thing that mattered; better a Leviathan than a social model in which decisions were made democratically (Hobbes 2009).

6. Honesty is the trait most highly valued in Sweden's national politicians. In a survey undertaken in 2000, 97 percent of Swedish respondents answered that honesty was a very or fairly important trait in a politician (Hvitfelt and Nord 2000).

7. In the 1998 national election, the electoral system was changed to allow personal voting that could alter the order of party lists. However, the effects have been rather small (Oscarsson and Holmberg 2013:268).

8. The 1998 Parliamentary Study was included as a sub-study in the evaluation of the element of preference voting that debuted on the national stage that year. The survey was distributed to about 1,000 candidates to the parliament and was carried out by the Department of Political Science at the University of Gothenburg under the direction of Martin Brothén and Sören Holmberg. The survey question from which the answer was derived read, "Generally speaking, what do you think of preference voting in connection with Swedish parliamentary elections?"

9. Svend Dahl (2011) shows that party members are schooled early on to adopt an attitude of disapproval toward political ambition. People who appear overtly interested in positions risk being dismissed as careerists.

10. The Parliamentary Studies have generated several publications, including Brothén and Holmberg, eds. 2010; Dahlström and Esaiasson 2013; Esaiasson and Holmberg 1996; Hagevi 1998; Holmberg 1974, 1997, 2003, 2006, 2010; Öhberg and Wängnerud 2014; Oskarson and Wängnerud 1995; and Wängnerud 1998, 2015.

CHAPTER 2. POLITICAL AMBITION THEORY

1. The book was written in the 1930s but not published in the United States until 1967, where it met with scathing criticism. See, for example, Erik Erikson's review in the *New York Review of Books*.

2. Freud did not develop any original theories about ambition, but, according to some scholars, in the early days of psychoanalysis ambition as such could be related to how the individual handled his Oedipus complex (Leib 1990:114). As a matter of curiosity, it can be mentioned that Freud believed there was a connection between urethral erotism and competitiveness (Haslam 2012).

3. Interest in questions related to political careers and ambition is not the sole province of American political scientists. Scholars in fields such as business administration and organizational studies have a long history of studying what it takes to achieve a successful career in business. Researchers have approached the question from different directions and a variety of perspectives. According to the meta-analysis carried out by Ng et al. (2005), there are four main predictors of career attainment. The first is human capital, which refers to individuals' educational, personal, and professional experiences. The second predictor concerns organizational sponsorship, where the crux is whether there is access to training and skills development opportunities, sponsorship from senior-level employees, etc., within the organization. The third predictor has to do with sociodemographic factors: gender, race, marital status, and age. The fourth predictor, stable individual differences, concerns dispositional traits and their relationship to career attainment. Generally speaking, it can be said that white men who are married, hardworking, and sponsored by their organizations are successful in their careers. The results are perhaps not destined to surprise, but it may be

somewhat more apparent that it can be proven that individual personality can be related to career attainment. Conscientious people are more successful, for instance, than people who are empathetic and friendly. Unstable individuals are the least successful (ibid). Increasing mobility in the labor market has also affected research in this area. Research was formerly preoccupied with why people change jobs and workplaces (see, e.g., Arthur and Rousseau 1996), but in recent years scholars have begun looking at why many people choose to stay at their workplace even though they have an opportunity to switch to a better job (see, e.g., Holtom and O'Neill 2004). In somewhat simplified terms, there seem to be three reasons that people choose to stay: the job fits with other aspects in their life space, they have strong links with their coworkers, and the sacrifice it would entail to break links with coworkers and change their current lives is too great (ibid.). Within this research, there is also ongoing discussion of why women have been less successful than men (Fels 2004; Konrad et al. 2000). Just as we have been able to observe a convergence in men's and women's political aspirations, the same tendency has been observed in working life in general (see, e.g., Schoon, Ross, and Martin 2007). The research still indicates lingering differences between boys and girls with regard to lofty career aspirations, where girls are more dependent than boys upon their family and social background for expressing aspirations for professional advancement, and where girls are less interested in challenging jobs. In contrast, parents had higher expectations and aspirations for teenage daughters than teenage sons (Ashby and Schoon 2010). Scholars have used both objective and subjective measures to study career attainment. The objective indicators are the pay and status an individual holds whereas the subjective measures are oriented toward how individuals assess their own attainments (Ng et al. 2005). Ng et al. argued in their overview that the two dimensions should be decoupled and assessed individually, as the same predictors are not always able to explain objective and subjective career attainment. Despite the wealth of research in this field, there is still a lack of clarity concerning how ambition should be defined and measured. We do not know, for instance, whether ambition is a cause or consequence of career attainment and opportunities (Dikkers, Van Engen, and Vinkenburg 2010:563).

4. There have, however, been at least some studies of progressive ambition within the EU Parliament, for example, Meserve, Pemstein, and Bernhard 2009; Scarrow 1997; Sieberer and Müller 2015.

5. Schlesinger says the same thing in a work published long afterward (1994), in which he referred with a certain pride to all the research inspired by his own study of 1966.

6. When Gordon Black published his study in 1972, rational choice theory had yet to make its breakthrough. Black thus felt compelled to explain, "The assumption of rationality, although generally accepted in economics, still provokes a strongly negative reaction among many political scientists, largely, it appears, because they do not understand the technical use of the term, as in game theory" (1972:145).

7. Studies of the Swedish parliament show that female MPs tend to pursue different issues than male MPs. Social care and services are higher on the agenda for female MPs (Wängnerud 1998). Subsequent research, however, has argued that the gap between men and women concerning which issues they prioritize has narrowed (Wängnerud 2015).

8. As a result, researchers have gone so far as to start "candidate schools" for young

women in order to ignite their political ambitions (see http://www.american.edu/spa/wpi/welead.cfm).

9. See, for example, Whistler and Ellickson's (2010:37n15) list of response frequencies in various survey studies of American politicians.

10. Candidates from Finland were also included in the study.

11. Otherwise, readers of Tage Erlander's memoirs, as in the other cases, will be reassured that he was never interested in a political career or driven by cravings for power. The interesting thing about Erlander's memoirs is that they are both personal and very frank. Still, the absence of personal career ambition is palpable, even though he managed to hold on as prime minister for twenty-three years.

12. It can be difficult to determine what should be regarded as realistic. If a person with a black father from Kenya and a white mother (who later remarried a Muslim man from Indonesia) were to decide he wanted to be president of the United States, it might seem to be evidence of poor grounding in reality.

13. There are different ways of studying MPs' career ambitions. One alternative would be to regard career ambition as something one can have a little or a lot of—that is, to presume that ambition is something that moves along a sliding scale. Ambition has not, however, been used in that way within this research discipline. In order to maintain dialogues with my international colleagues, I have chosen to adapt the study to make it as translatable as possible to international standards.

CHAPTER 3. ARE THERE MPS WHO ASPIRE TO HIGH POSITIONS?

1. In 1988, Minister of Justice Anna-Greta Leijon was actually promised a cabinet position in Ingvar Carlsson's government. The promise was given in connection with Leijon's resignation (in the aftermath of a political scandal). Nonetheless, Leijon was passed over after the 1988 election (Leijon 1991).

2. The first MEPs were appointed by their parties when Sweden acceded to the EU (then the EC) in January 1995. A national election to the European Parliament was held that September.

3. The definition also included the MP's level of job satisfaction in the parliament, but the question is not especially critical because more than 90 percent of MPs in the 1996 study reported that they were happy (44 percent) or very happy (50 percent) in the parliament.

4. There may be reason to explain why I use statistical significance in relation to a total sample. First, this is a widely accepted method among parliamentary scholars; see, for example, Esaiasson and Holmberg 1996; Martin 2011; Searing 1994. Second, and more important, this allows me to gain an understanding of the robustness of the results. I will borrow my justification from Jörgen Hermansson: "Partly, it is a kind of insurance against the effects of isolated coding errors, and partly a guarantee that our findings are in fact manifestations of empirical patterns and not merely more randomly generated connections" (Ahlbäck Öberg, Hermansson, and Wängnerud 2007:30n17).

5. At the same time, we cannot help but notice that nearly 40 percent of first-term MPs

have hopes or aspirations for more prominent positions within and outside of the parliament.

CHAPTER 4. WHICH MPS ASPIRE TO HIGH POSITIONS?

1. When the discussion has revolved around ambition and socioeconomic status, it has dealt with citizens and their political plans for the future (see, e.g., Lawless and Fox 2010; Fulton et al. 2006). But thus far there are no studies concerning the socioeconomic status and career ambitions of the political elite.

2. There is no major difference in the level of interest in political office between native-born (16 percent) and foreign-born (13 percent) citizens. This is the case even though immigrants are not as active in the political parties and represent a smaller percentage of elected representatives (Petersson 1998).

3. No distinct gender differences are shown in the study by Verba, Schlozman, and Brady. Political participation may vary somewhat in nature depending upon the activity, but the differences are not striking (see Verba, Schlozman and Brady 1995, chapter 8). With respect to women's representation in national parliaments, however, only 18 percent of the world's national parliamentarians are women; Scandinavia is an important exception (Wängnerud 2009).

4. Between 1921 and 1970 Sweden had a total of five female cabinet ministers. Sweden's first woman minister was Karin Kock, who took office in 1947.

5. Social scientists have increasingly begun studying how wages and other benefits of the office affect the supply of skilled candidates (see, e.g., Diermeier, Keane, and Merlo 2005). However, there is some lack of consensus as to whether wage levels influence the quality of candidates and policy content (compare, for example, the conclusions of Keane and Merlo 2007 with those of Ferraz and Finan 2008). A Finnish study has shown that a substantial increase in the wages of parliamentarians resulted in more highly educated women entering the parliament (Kotakorpi and Poutvaara 2010).

6. The definition is established within the framework of the Parliamentary Studies (e.g., Esaiasson and Holmberg 1996) and was introduced in Holmberg 1974:276.

7. Compare this to John Aldrich, for example, who in *Why Parties?* (1995) argues that individuals start parties because they want to realize their own political ambitions. That thesis has been tested in Sweden and found wrong (Erlingsson 2005).

8. The background variables are the same as in the first regression model and where the other factors are held at their respective average values. Using the margins command (Stata 12).

CHAPTER 5. ARE THERE MPS WITH REAL CAREER AMBITIONS?

1. One of the reasons for the attention was that when Gahrton defended his thesis, the grading committee disagreed about whether the thesis should be accepted. Two members wanted to pass the thesis while two others held the opposite opinion. Gahrton's adviser had

the deciding vote, however, and green-lighted the thesis. Due to this situation having arisen, a majority of the grading committee is no longer allowed to be from the same department as the doctoral candidate. The rule became known as "Lex Gahrton."

2. *Fokus* magazine, "Politicians Are Fleeing to Brussels," 29 May 2009.

3. Things sometimes go wrong despite the best of intentions. One old-timer in Congress likes to tell the story of a freshman senator who joined his more senior colleagues in paying tribute to an older senator on his birthday. The birthday boy did not appreciate the freshman's laudatory speech, and loudly whispered to his neighbor, "That son-of-a-bitch, that son-of-a-bitch." He did not dislike the freshman personally—it was just that he was a freshman and as such should hold his tongue (Matthews 1959:1066).

4. The quotation was taken from a paper included in a book Matthews published the following year.

5. There is, however, research that contradicts Manin's argument and argues that the thesis that politics is going to become more focused on the individual is exaggerated (see, e.g., Karvonen 2010; King 2002).

6. The need to establish a personal reputation also recurs when researchers study who achieves career attainment in ordinary working life (Cooper, Graham, and Dyke 1993).

7. The idea of representation goes back to the Middle Ages, when there were discussions of the rights of popes and monarchs to exert power. The notion that the ruler is dependent upon the consent of the people arose out of the ensuing disagreements. Before then, the ruler had gained legitimacy through the belief in divine ordainment (Ullman cited in Pollak 2007:95ff). However, obtaining a mandate does not mean that someone must bow to the wishes of the mandate-giver. The holder of royal power curried favor with his subjects so that their consent was expressed in an open mandate (Rehfeld 2009).

8. It is also possible to contrast the MPs' relative lack of interest in their own constituencies by comparing it to their interest in other geographical units. In a set of questions that concerned the MPs' "interest in politics in other countries/regions," including their own constituencies, the Nordic region, the Baltic countries, and the EU, there were significant differences in eight out of twelve cases in the question set. In seven of the cases, potentially ambitious MPs *were more* interested in politics in other regions/countries, except when it came to "own constituency/region"—where they reported *less* interest.

9. There is also reason to consider the direction of the correlation between "vulnerability" and work in the home constituency. When I interviewed a number of MPs and asked them how an MP should behave to achieve success in the parliament, one MP said, "You have to be able to shed the mantle of the home district. Not everyone can. They get stuck and cannot move on. . . . They do not keep up." What the MP is essentially saying is that MPs who focus too much on their home constituencies are regarded by their colleagues as someone with a relatively limited repertoire.

10. The conditions for the analysis are the same as in Table 5.1, using the margins command (Stata 12).

11. In Edmund Burke's case, this meant that he set himself in opposition to public opinion in Bristol, which wanted to institute trade barriers against Ireland. In so doing, his fate was sealed.

12. The quotation was taken from "The Founders' Constitution," http://presspubs.uchi cago.edu/founders/documents/v1ch13s7.html

13. There is another question from the Parliamentary Studies that concerned which social groups the MPs believe it is important to represent. Among potentially ambitious MPs, 37 percent answered that it is very important to represent "Everyone in Sweden." The corresponding figure for other MPs is 21 percent.

14. In Table 5.4, we could see that only 5 percent of the MPs want to strengthen party discipline and that none want to strengthen the norms related to compliance with the party line. If we more specifically study the MPs' attitudes toward the norms related to the party line, it proves that 18 percent of the potential career politicians believe the party line should be less strict. The corresponding figure for the other group is 8 percent. The difference is significant (**).

15. The conditions for the analysis are the same as in Tables 5.1, 5.2, and 5.3.

16. When the Republicans managed to take control of Congress in 1994 and come back after Bill Clinton's victory in 1992, one of the actions they took was to reinforce party discipline. One way of showing the voters that the Republicans were a united force was to enter into a "Contract with America" six weeks before the congressional election. The contract contained detailed election promises of what would happen if the Republicans won the election. Presenting a united front ahead of the election proved to be a competitive advantage. The Republicans ended up in control of both houses of Congress for the first time in 40 years (Woodward 1996).

17. American researchers have also pointed out that women politicians have been nominated by their parties in elections the parties cannot win, and were thus put forward as sacrificial lambs (Carroll 1994).

18. Potentially ambitious MPs, however, do not ascribe any particular importance to good relationships with the mass media in order to influence the party—in this respect, the numbers are higher among the other MPs. Of the latter, 12 percent consider relationships with the mass media very important.

19. Potentially ambitious MPs also give greater consideration to the leadership of the parliament party group, but only if the option "Great consideration" is set against the other options; that is, if the variable is made two-tailed. The same applies when one asks the MPs who they listen to when they form their ideas.

CHAPTER 6. ARE AMBITIOUS MPS SUCCESSFUL?

1. In the early 1970s Donald Searing initiated a project aimed at describing the roles of politicians in the British parliament. To complete the task, Searing aimed to interview all 630 British parliamentarians, of whom 521 agreed to be interviewed. The study design was very ambitious. In addition to the interviews, the MPs were asked to respond to surveys and accept participatory observations by Searing. It took almost two years just to conduct the interviews, and twenty years for the final product to be published (Searing 1994). Searing's reward for his labors were the interesting results that helped give role theories a new theo-

retical framework (Strøm 1997). Searing's study is unique; nothing similar has been done since.

2. Please note that "seniority" has been eliminated from the regression on Table 6.1 due to the risk of multicollinearity. The variables on the MPs' tenure in the parliament, current age, age upon first election to the parliament, and number of years since joining the party are closely aligned. In the main, the results shown in Table 6.1 do not change, other than that the explained variance declines. The MPs' current age is eliminated from the regression that examines how old the MPs were upon first election to the parliament. This was done because a young MP could not have been anything other than young when first elected to the parliament. This procedure does not affect the main results either.

3. It took women about sixteen years to make it to the parliament; men took on average three years longer. The same conditions apply at the local government level. The women's advantage also applies to MPs with an academic background. On average, there is a difference of slightly more than four years (sixteen versus twenty-one years, respectively) between those who are university educated and those who are not.

4. I have had no opportunity to follow developments because subsequent Parliamentary Studies did not ask the MPs when they joined their parties, but there is no difference in the 1994 parliament between newcomer women and more senior women.

5. Fredrik Reinfeldt was twenty-six, and Carl Bildt and Göran Persson were thirty. Tage Erlander, Olof Palme, and Ingvar Carlsson were thirty-one. Per Albin Hansson and Torbjörn Fälldin were thirty-two, and Ola Ullsten was thirty-four.

6. Even though Gustav Möller made no secret of his unhappiness with the election of Tage Erlander, Erlander sympathized with Möller. On the human level, Erlander expresses pity that one of his best friends was "falling apart right in front of me" (Erlander 2001:150).

7. In *Representation from Above* Esaiasson and Holmberg tested the importance of various types of scoring systems to assess the MPs' career attainment. The tests of the various systems showed that they had no significant effect on the assessment of the results that emerged in their study (Esaiasson and Holmberg 1996:40).

8. The difference remains if we follow the MPs for an additional term (2010–2014), when 20 percent of ambitious MPs were still in the parliament while only 4 percent of the other MPs had retained their seats.

9. The conditions for the analysis are the same as in Table 6.5. Using the margins command (Stata 12).

10. The data on the MPs' status were taken from the Swedish parliament's biographical series Fakta om Folkvalda, which has been published after every general election since the 1982–1985 term in office.

11. In *Exit Riksdagen*, the scores were computed in a different way. The positions were roughly the same as in this study and had a corresponding average score of 0.5 (2007:41).

12. Please note that "status" as an independent variable has been eliminated from the regression on Table 6.7.

CHAPTER 7. IS SWEDEN DIFFERENT?

1. Belgium 58 percent, France 25 percent, Germany 47 percent, Greece 20 percent, Ireland 43 percent, Italy 15 percent, Luxembourg 47 percent, Netherlands 43 percent, Portugal 24 percent, Spain 37 percent, and Sweden 90 percent.

2. The data set is described in greater detail in Katz and Wessels 1999:250–251. A test using the Duncan Socioeconomic Index showed that the level of representation of the respondents for each country with regard to gender, party, and age was sufficient in most of the countries.

3. Other scholars argue that the reverse is true. Closed lists instead encourage politicians to develop concerns for the reputation of the party as a whole. The politicians have no need to establish personal political reputations and thus do not need money to finance their campaigns. As a result, they are less likely to succumb to corruption (Chang and Golden 2007).

4. The notion that the political culture is a crucial component of a political system has been argued as far back as Aristotle (Welzel 2009). Aristotle held that the beliefs of a predominant group also form the basis of the political system's legitimacy. It was for this reason, according to Aristotle, that democracy was dependent upon the existence of a large middle class. The moderating beliefs of the middle class gave the political system stability and legitimacy (ibid).

CHAPTER 8. AMBITION IN REPRESENTATIVE DEMOCRACY

1. One should not, however, be overly cautious, as reflected in an Israeli study of political ambition. The lead researcher points out in the method section of the paper that certain difficulties are attached to the choice of subject as such. "An initial problem was found in the national political culture, which discourages overt expression of political aspirations and instead directs that 'the office seeks the man'" (Pomper 1975:716ff). For this reason, the researchers chose not to ask any explicit questions about the politicians' career aspirations. The questions instead had to do with whether the respondents would be willing to continue in public life, if they would be willing to be a candidate for the Knesset, and if they would be willing even if they did not have a realistic place on the party list. This way of circumventing the core issue of political career ambition is perhaps unsuitable if the research interest is in fact ambition. As the author states in his conclusions, "a better measure of ambition is also needed" (ibid., 731).

BIBLIOGRAPHY

Aars, Jacob. 1997. *Rekruttering og personskifte i lokalpolitikken: en sammenligning av Finland og Norge*. Bergen: Institutt for sosiologi of statsvitenskapelige fag, Senter for mediaforskning.

Aars, Jacob, and Audun Offerdal. 1998. "Local Political Recruitment in Crisis? A Comparison of Finland and Norway." *Scandinavian Political Studies* 21(3): 207–230.

Abramson, Paul R., John H. Aldrich, and David W. Rohde. 1987. "Progressive Ambition among United States Senators: 1972–1988." *Journal of Politics* 49:3–35.

Adelsohn, Ulf. 1987. *Partiledare: dagbok 1981–1986*. Malmö: Gedins.

Ahlbäck Öberg, Shirin, Jörgen Hermansson, and Lena Wängnerud. 2007. *Exit Riksdagen*. Malmö: Liber.

Aldrich, John H. 1995. *Why Parties?* Chicago: University of Chicago Press.

Alford, John R., Carolyn L. Funk, and John R. Hibbing. 2005. "Are Political Orientations Genetically Transmitted?" *American Political Science Review* 99(2):153–168.

Aquilino, William S. 1994. "Interview Mode Effects in Surveys of Drug and Alcohol Use." *Public Opinion Quarterly* 58(2):210–240.

Aristotle. 2009. *The Nicomachean Ethics*. Oxford: Oxford University Press.

Arthur, Michael Bernard, and Denise M. Rousseau, eds. 1996. *The Boundaryless Career: A New Employment Principle for a New Organizational Era*. Oxford: Oxford University Press.

Ashby, Julie S., and Ingrid Schoon. 2010. "Career Success: The Role of Teenage Career Aspirations, Ambition Value and Gender in Predicting Adult Social Status and Earnings." *Journal of Vocational Behavior* 77(3): 350–360.

Atkinson, Anthony Barnes, Lee Rainwater, and Timothy M. Smeeding. 1995. *Income Distribution in the OECD Countries: The Evidence from the Luxembourg Income Study*. Paris: Organization for Economic Cooperation and Development.

Bäck, Hanna, et al. 2007. *Från statsminister till president? Sveriges regeringschef i ett jämförande perspektiv*. Swedish Government Report SOU 2007:42. Stockholm: Fritzes.

Banks, Jeffrey S., and D. Roderick Kiewiet. 1989. "Explaining Patterns of Candidate Competition in Congressional Elections." *American Journal of Political Science* 33(4):997–1015.

Barber, James David. 1985. *The Presidential Character: Predicting Performance in the White House*. Englewood Cliffs, NJ: Prentice Hall.

Barrling Hermansson, Katarina. 2004. *Partikulturer Kollektiva självbilder och normer i Sveriges riksdag*. Uppsala: Uppsala University.

Bell, Charles G., and Charles M. Price. 1969. "Pre-Legislative Sources of Representational Roles." *Midwest Journal of Political Science* 13(2):254–270.

Besley, Timothy, Torsten Persson, and Daniel M. Sturm. 2010. "Political Competition, Policy, and Growth: Theory and Evidence from the United States." *Review of Economic Studies* 77(4):1329–1352.

Black, Gordon S. 1972. "A Theory of Political Ambition: Career Choices and the Role of Structural Incentives." *American Political Science Review* 66:144–159.

Bodström, Lennart. 2001. *Mitt i stormen*. Stockholm: Hjalmarson and Högberg.

Boehm, Christopher. 2008. "Purposive Social Selection and the Evolution of Human Altruism." *Cross-Cultural Research* 42(4):319–352.

Bogaert, Sandy, Christophe Boone, and Carolyn Declerck. 2008. "Social Value Orientation and Cooperation in Social Dilemmas: A Review and Conceptual Model." *British Journal of Social Psychology* 47(3):453–480.

Bohman, Gösta. 1983. *Så var det*. Stockholm: Bonniers.

Borchert, Jens. 2003. "The Political Class in Advanced Democracies: Towards a Comparative Perspective." In Jens Borchert and Jürgen Zeiss, eds., *The Political Class in Advanced Democracies*. Oxford: Oxford University Press.

Borchert, Jens, and Klaus Stolz. 2011. "Introduction: Political Careers in Multi-level Systems." *Regional and Federal Studies* 21(2):107–115.

Box-Steffensmeier, Janet M., et al. 2003. "The Effects of Political Representation on the Electoral Advantages of House Incumbents." *Political Research Quarterly* 56(3):259–270.

Brace, Paul. 1984. "Progressive Ambition in the House: A Probabilistic Approach." *Journal of Politics* 46:556–571.

Bratton, Kathleen A., and Kerry L. Haynie. 1999. "Agenda Setting and Legislative Success in State Legislatures: The Effects of Gender and Race." *Journal of Politics* 61:658–679.

Brothén, Martin, and Sören Holmberg, eds. 2010. *Folkets representanter*. Gothenburg: Department of Political Science, University of Gothenburg.

Burke, Edmund. 1774. "Speech to the Electors of Bristol." http://press-pubs.uchicago.edu/founders/documents/v1ch13s7.html.

Cain, Bruce E., John Ferejohn, and Morris Fiorina. 1987. *The Personal Vote: Constituency Service and Electoral Independence*. Cambridge, MA: Harvard University Press.

Cain, Bruce E., and Thad Kousser. 2004. *Adaption to Term Limits: Recent Experiences and New Directions*. San Francisco: Public Policy Institute of California.

Canon, David T. 1990. *Actors, Athletes, and Astronauts: Political Amateurs in the United States Congress*. Chapel Hill: University of North Carolina Press.

———. 1993. "Sacrificial Lambs or Strategic Politicians? Political Amateurs in US House Elections." *American Journal of Political Science* 37(4):1119–1141.

Caprara, Gian Vittorio, et al. 2003. "Personalities of Politicians and Voters: Unique and Synergistic Relationships." *Journal of Personality and Social Psychology* 84(4):849–856.

Carey, John M., and Matthew Soberg Shugart. 1995. "Incentives to Cultivate a Personal Vote: A Rank Ordering of Electoral Formulas." *Electoral Studies* 14(4):417–439.

Carey, John M., et al. 2006. "The Effects of Term Limits on State Legislatures: A New Survey of the 50 States." *Legislative Studies Quarterly* 31(1):105–134.

Carroll, Susan J. 1994. *Women as Candidates in American Politics*. Bloomington: Indiana University Press.

Carson, Jamie L. 2005. "Strategy, Selection, and Candidate Competition in House and Senate Elections." *Journal of Politics* 67(1):1–46.

Caul, Miki. 1999. "Women's Representation in Parliament: The Role of Political Parties." *Party Politics* 5(1):79–98.

Chang, Eric C.C., and Miriam A. Golden. 2007. "Electoral Systems, District Magnitude, and Corruption." *British Journal of Political Science* 37(1):115–137.

Codispoti, Frank. 1982. *American Governors and Progressive Ambition: An Analysis of Opportunities to Run for the Senate.* Ph.D. diss., Michigan State University.

Cooper, William H., William J. Graham, and Lorraine S. Dyke. 1993. "Tournament Players." In Gerald R. Ferris, ed., *Research in Personnel and Human Resource Management.* Greenwich, CT: JAI Press.

Cox, Gary W. 1987. *The Efficient Secret.* New York: Cambridge University Press.

Cox, Gary W., and Mathew D. McCubbins. 1993. *Legislative Leviathan: Party Government in the House.* Berkeley: University of California Press.

———. 2007. *Legislative Leviathan: Party Government in the House,* 2nd ed. Cambridge: Cambridge University Press.

Cross, William, and Lisa Young. 2008. "Factors Influencing the Decision of the Young Politically Engaged to Join a Political Party." *Party Politics* 14(3):345–369.

Crowe, Edward. 1983. "Consensus and Structure in Legislative Norms: Party Discipline in the House of Commons." *Journal of Politics* 45:907–931.

Dahl, Svend. 2011. *Efter folkrörelsepartiet.* Stockholm: Stockholm University.

Dahlström, Carl, and Peter Esaiasson. 2013. "The Immigration Issue and Anti-Immigrant Party Success in Sweden, 1970–2006: A Deviant Case Analysis." *Party Politics* 19(2):343–364.

Dal Bó, Ernesto, Pedro Dal Bó, and Jason Snyder. 2009. "Political Dynasties." *Review of Economic Studies* 76(1):115–142.

Davidson, Roger H. 1969. *The Role of the Congressman.* New York: Pegasus.

Davidsson, Lars. 2006. *I linje med partiet? Maktspel och lojalitet i den svenska Riksdagen.* Stockholm: SNS Förlag.

Dawes, Christopher T., et al. 2007. "Egalitarian Motives in Humans." *Nature* 446:794–796.

De Cremer, David, and Daan Van Knippenberg. 2004. "Leader Self-Sacrifice and Leadership Effectiveness: The Moderating Role of Leader Self-Confidence." *Organizational Behavior and Human Decision Processes* 95(2):140–155.

Deininger, Klaus, and Lyn Squire. 1996. "A New Data Set Measuring Income Inequality." *World Bank Economic Review* 10(3):565–591.

Diamond, Jared. 1997. *Guns, Germs, and Steel: The Fate of Human Societies.* New York: W. W. Norton.

Diermeier, Daniel, Michael Keane, and Antonio Merlo. 2005. "A Political Economy Model of Congressional Careers." *American Economic Review* 95(1):347–373.

Dikkers, Josje, Marloes van Engen, and Claartje Vinkenburg. 2010. "Flexible Work: Ambitious Parents' Recipe for Career Success in the Netherlands." *Career Development International* 15(6):562–582.

Downs, Anthony. 1957. *An Economic Theory of Democracy.* New York: Harper and Row.

Duverger, Maurice. 1954. *Political Parties: Their Organization and Activities in the Modern State.* London: Methuen.

Eagly, Alice H., Mona G. Makhijani, and Bruce G. Klonsky. 1992. "Gender and the Evaluation of Leaders: A Meta-Analysis." *Psychological Bulletin* 111(1):3–22.

Ehrenhalt, Alan. 1991. *The United States of Ambition: Politicians, Power, and the Pursuit of Office.* New York: Random House.

Elazar, Daniel J. 1966. *American Federalism: A View from the States.* New York: Crowell.

Engstrom, Richard L. 1971. "Political Ambition and the Prosecutorial Office." *Journal of Politics* 33:190–194.

Erikson, Erik. 1967. "The Strange Case of Freud, Bullitt, and Woodrow Wilson." *New York Review of Books* (3).

Erlander, Tage. 2001. *Dagböcker 1945–1949.* Published by Sven Erlander. Hedemora: Gidlund Förlag.

Erlingsson, Gissur. 2005. *Varför bildas nya partier.* Lund: Lund University.

Esaiasson, Peter, and Sören Holmberg. 1996. *Representation from Above: Members of Parliament and Representative Democracy in Sweden.* Dartmouth, UK: Aldershot.

Eulau, Heinz, and Kenneth Prewitt. 1973. *Labyrinths of Democracy: Adaptations, Linkages, Representation, and Policies in Urban Politics.* Indianapolis: Bobbs-Merrill.

Eulau, Heinz, and John C. Wahlke. 1978. *The Politics of Representation: Continuities in Theory and Research.* London: Sage.

Eulau, Heinz, et al. 1959. "The Role of the Representative: Some Empirical Observations on the Theory of Edmund Burke." *American Political Science Review* 53(3):742–756.

Fakta om folkvalda. 1998.*The Riksdag, 1994–1998.* Stockholm: Swedish Riksdag.

———. 2010. *The Riksdag, 2006–2010.* Stockholm: Swedish Riksdag.

Faulkner, Robert. 2007. *The Case for Greatness.* New Haven, CT: Yale University Press.

Federley, Fredrick. 2010. *Bara jag.* Stocksund: Hydra.

Fehr, Ernst, Urs Fischbacher, and Simon Gächter. 2002. "Strong Reciprocity, Human Cooperation, and the Enforcement of Social Norms." *Human Nature* 13(1):1–25.

Feldman, Paul, and James Jondrow. 1984. "Congressional Elections and Local Federal Spending." *American Journal of Political Science* 28(1):147–164.

Fels, Anna. 2004. "Do Women Lack Ambition?" *Harvard Business Review* 82(4):50–60.

Fenno, Richard F. 1978. *Home Style: House Members in Their Districts.* Boston: Little, Brown.

———. 1996. *Senators on the Campaign Trail: The Politics of Representation.* Norman: University of Oklahoma Press.

Ferraz, Claudio, and Frederico Finan. 2008. "Motivating Politicians: The Impacts of Monetary Incentives on Quality and Performance." *Mimeo.* 2009 NBER Working Paper 14906.

Fichtelius, Erik. 2007. *Aldrig ensam, alltid ensam: Samtalen med Göran Persson 1996–2006.* Stockholm: Norstedts.

Flanigan, William H., and Nancy H. Zingale. 2002. *Political Behavior of the American Electorate,* 10th ed. Washington, DC: CQ Press.

Fowler, James H., and Darren Schreiber. 2008. "Biology, Politics, and the Emerging Science of Human Nature." *Science* 322(5903):912–914.

Fowler, Linda L. 1993. *Candidates, Congress, and the American Democracy.* Ann Arbor: University of Michigan Press.

Fowler, Linda L., and Robert D. McClure. 1989. *Political Ambition: Who Decides to Run for Congress?* New Haven, CT: Yale University Press.

Fox, Richard. L. 2000. "Gender and Congressional Elections." In Sue Tolleson-Rinehart and Jyl J. Josephson, eds., *Gender and American Politics: Women, Men, and the Political Process.* Armonk, NY: M.E. Sharpe.

Fox, Richard L., and Jennifer L. Lawless. 2010. "If Only They'd Ask: Gender, Recruitment, and Political Ambition." *Journal of Politics* 72(02):310–326.

Fox, Richard L., Jennifer L. Lawless, and Courtney Feeley. 2001. "Gender and the Decision to Run for Office." *Legislative Studies Quarterly* 26(3):411–435.

Francis, Wayne L., and Lawrence W. Kenny. 1996. "Position Shifting in Pursuit of Higher Office." *American Journal of Political Science* 40(3):768–786.

———. 2000. *Up the Political Ladder.* Thousand Oaks, CA: Sage.

Freeman, Jo. 1986. "The Political Culture of the Democratic and Republican Parties." *Political Science Quarterly* 101(3):327–356.

Freidenvall, Lenita. 2006. *Vägen till Varannan damernas: Om kvinnorepresentation, kvotering och kandidaturval i svensk politik 1970–2002.* Stockholm: Stockholm Studies in Politics.

Freud, Sigmund, and William C. Bullitt. 1999. *Thomas Woodrow Wilson: A Psychological Study.* Boston: Houghton Mifflin.

Fuchs, Dieter. 2007. "The Political Culture Paradigm." In Russel J. Dalton and Hans-Dieter Klingemann., eds., *The Oxford Handbook of Political Behavior.* Oxford: Oxford University Press.

Fulton, Sarah A., et al. 2006. "The Sense of a Woman: Gender, Ambition, and the Decision to Run for Congress." *Political Research Quarterly* 59(2):235–248.

Gaddie, Ronald Keith. 2004. *Born to Run: Origins of the Political Career.* Lanham, MD: Rowman and Littlefield.

Gaddie, Ronald Keith, and Charles S. Bullock. 2000. *Elections to Open Seats in the US House: Where the Action Is.* Lanham, MD: Rowman and Littlefield.

Gahrton, Per. 1983. *Riksdagen inifrån: En studie av parlamentarisk handfallenhet inför ett samhälle i kris.* Stockholm: Prisma.

Gallagher, Michael. 1991. "Proportionality, Disproportionality, and Electoral Systems." *Electoral Studies* 10(1):33–51.

Gidlund, Gullan, and Tommy Möller. 1999. *Demokratins trotjänare: Lokalt partiarbete förr och nu.* Swedish Government Report SOU 1999:130. Stockholm: Fakta info.direkt.

Gilljam, Mikael. 2003. "Deltagardemokrati med förhinder." In Mikael Gilljam and Jörgen Hermansson, eds., *Demokratins mekanismer.* Lund: Studentlitteratur.

Graubard, Stephen R., ed. 1986. *Norden—The Passion for Equality.* Oslo: Norwegian University Press.

Haeberle, Steven H. 1985. "Closed Primaries and Party Support in Congress." *American Politics Quarterly* 13:341–352.

Hagevi, Magnus. 1995. *Riksdagen utifrån: En gahrtonsk teori synas i sömmarna.* Gothenburg: Department of Political Science, University of Gothenburg.

———. 1998. *Bakom riksdagens fasad.* Gothenburg: Akademiförlaget Corona.

————. 2003. "Sweden: Between Participation Ideal and Professionalism." In Jens Borchert and Jürgen Zeiss, eds., *The Political Class in Advanced Democracies: A Comparative Handbook.* Oxford: Oxford University Press.

————. 2009. *Politisk opinion och religiositet i Västra Götaland.* Lund: Sekel.

————. 2010. "Anciennitetsprincipens uppgång och fall." In Martin Brothén and Sören Holmberg, eds., *Folkets representanter: En bok om riksdagsledmöterna och politisk representation i Sverige.* Gothenburg: Department of Political Science, University of Gothenburg.

Hardy, Charlie L., and Mark Van Vugt. 2006. "Nice Guys Finish First: The Competitive Altruism Hypothesis." *Personality and Social Psychology Bulletin* 32(10):1402–1413.

Haslam, Nick. 2012. *Psychology in the Bathroom.* New York: Palgrave Macmillan.

Hatemi, Peter K., et al. 2007. "The Genetics of Voting: An Australian Twin Study." *Behavior Genetics* 37(3):435–448.

Hermansson, Jörgen, et al. 2010. *Regeringsmakten i Sverige: Ett experiment i parlamentarism 1917–2009.* Stockholm: SNS Förlag.

Herrick, Rebekah. 2001. "The Effects of Political Ambition on Legislative Behavior: A Replication." *Social Science Journal* 38(3):469–474.

Herrick, Rebekah, and Samuel H. Fisher. 2007. *Representing America: The Citizen and the Professional Legislators in the House of Representatives.* Plymouth, UK: Lexington Books.

Herrick, Rebekah, and Michael K. Moore. 1993. "Political Ambition's Effect on Legislative Behavior: Schlesinger's Typology Reconsidered and Revised." *Journal of Politics* 55(3): 765–776.

Hibbing, John R. 1986. "Ambition in the House: Behavioral Consequences of Higher Office Goals among US Representatives." *American Journal of Political Science* 30:651–665.

Hobbes, Thomas. 2009. *Leviathan.* Oxford: Oxford University Press.

Holmberg, Sören. 1974. *Riksdagens representerar svenska folket: Empiriska studier i representativ demokrati.* Lund: Studentlitteratur.

————. 1997. "Dynamic Opinion Representation." *Scandinavian Political Studies* 20:265–283.

————. 2003. "Are Political Parties Necessary?" *Electoral Studies* 22(3):287–300.

————. 2006. "Åsiktsrepresenterad." In Hanna Bäck and Mikael Gilljam, eds., *Valets Mekanismer.* Stockholm: Liber.

————. 2010. "Dynamic Representation from Above." In Martin Rosema, Bas Denters, and Kees Aarts, eds., *How Democracy Works: Political Representation and Policy Congruence in Modern Societies.* Amsterdam: Amsterdam University Press.

Holmberg, Sören, and Henrik Oscarsson. 2004. *Väljare: Svenskt väljarbeteende under 50 år.* Stockholm: Norstedts juridik.

Holtom, Brooks C., and Bonnie S. O'Neill. 2004. "Job Embeddedness: A Theoretical Foundation for Developing a Comprehensive Nurse Retention Plan." *Journal of Nursing Administration* 34(5):216–227.

Houser, Rollen Edward. 2002. "The Virtue of Courage." In Stephen J. Pope, ed., *The Ethics of Aquinas.* Georgetown, MD: Georgetown University Press.

Hvitfelt, Håkan, and Lars Nord. 2000. "Förlänger ett gott skratt politikerlivet?" In Sören

Holmberg and Lennart Weibull, eds., *Land du välsignade*. Gothenburg: SOM Institute, University of Gothenburg.

Immelman, Aubrey. 2003. "Personality in Political Psychology." In Irving B Weiner, Theodore Millon, and Melvin J. Lerner, eds., *Handbook of Psychology: Vol. 5, Personality and Social Psychology*. Hoboken, NJ: Wiley.

Inglehart, Ronald, and Pippa Norris. 2003. *Rising Tide: Gender Equality and Cultural Change around the World*. New York: Cambridge University Press.

Isaksson, Anders. 2002. *Den politiska adeln: politikens förvandling från uppdrag till yrke*. Stockholm: Wahlström and Widstrand.

Isberg, Magnus. 1999. *Riksdagsledamoten i sin partigrupp: 52 riksdagsveteraners erfarenheter av partigruppernas arbetssätt och inflytande*. Stockholm: Gidlunds Förlag.

Jacobson, Gary C. 1989. "Strategic Politicians and the Dynamics of US House Elections, 1946–86." *American Political Science Review* 83(3):773–794.

———. 2004. *The Politics of Congressional Elections*. New York: Pearson Longman.

Jacobson, Gary C., and Samuel Kernell. 1983. *Strategy and Choice in Congressional Elections*. New Haven, CT: Yale University Press.

Jensen, Torben. 2000. "Party Cohesion." In Peter Esaiasson and Knut Heidar, eds., *Beyond Westminster and Congress: The Nordic Experience*. Columbus: Ohio State University Press.

Johansson, Anders. 1992. *Gunnar Sträng: Landsvägsagitatorn*. Stockholm: Tidens Förlag.

Jordahl, Henrik. 2009. "Inequality and Trust." In Gert Svendsen Tinggaard and Gunnar Lind Haase Svendsen, eds., *Handbook of Social Capital: The Troika of Sociology, Political Science, and Economics*. Northampton, MA: Edward Elgar.

Karlsson, David. 2001. "Ny som förtroendevald i kommuner och landsting." *Att vara med på riktigt—demokratiutveckling i kommuner och landsting*. Swedish Government Report SOU 2001:48. Stockholm: Fritzes.

Karvonen, Lauri. 2010. *The Personalization of Politics: A Study of Parliamentary Democracies*. Essex: ECPR Press.

Katz, Richard S., and Peter Mair, eds. 1994. *How Parties Organize: Change and Adaptation in Party Organizations in Western Democracies*. London: Sage.

Katz, Richard S., and Bernhard Wessels, eds. 1999. *The European Parliament, the National Parliaments, and European Integration*. Oxford: Oxford University Press.

Kavanagh, Dennis. 1992. "Changes in the Political Class and Its Culture." *Parliamentary Affairs* 45(1):18–32.

Kazee, Thomas A., ed. 1994. *Who Runs for Congress? Ambition, Context, and Candidate Emergence*. Washington, DC: CQ Press.

Keane, Michael P., and Antonio Merlo. 2007. *Money, Political Ambition, and the Career Decisions of Politicians*. PIER Working Paper No. 07-016.

Kenworthy, Lane, and Melissa Malami. 1999. "Gender Inequality in Political Representation: A Worldwide Comparative Analysis." *Social Forces* 78(1):235–268.

Key, Valdimer Orlando. 1956. *American State Politics: An Introduction*. New York: Knopf.

Kiewiet, D. Roderick, and Mathew D. McCubbins. 1991. *The Logic of Delegation*. Chicago: University of Chicago Press.

Kinder, Donald R., et al. 1980. "Presidential Prototypes." *Political Behavior* 2(4):315–337.

King, Anthony. 2002. "Conclusions and Implications." In Anthony King, ed., *Leaders' Personalities and the Outcomes of Democratic Elections*. Oxford: Oxford University Press.

Kirkpatrick, Jeane J. 1976. *The New Presidential Elite*. New York: Russell Sage Foundation.

Kittilson, Miki Caul. 2006. *Challenging Parties, Changing Parliaments: Women and Elected Office in Contemporary Western Europe*. Columbus: Ohio State University Press.

Konrad, Alison M., et al. 2000. "Sex Differences and Similarities in Job Attribute Preferences: A Meta-Analysis." *Psychological Bulletin* 126(4):593–641.

Kornberg, Allan. 1967: *Canadian Legislative Behavior*. New York: Holt, Rinehart, and Winston.

Kotakorpi, Kaisa, and Panu Poutvaara. 2010. "Pay for Politicians and Candidate Selection: An Empirical Analysis." *Journal of Public Economics* 95(7-8):877–885.

Kousser, Thad. 2006. "The Limited Impact of Term Limits: Contingent Effects on the Complexity and Breadth of Laws." *State Politics and Policy Quarterly* 6(4):410–429.

Kunicová, Jana, and Susan Rose-Ackerman. 2005. "Electoral Rules and Constitutional Structure as Constraints on Corruption." *British Journal of Political Science* 35(4):573–606.

Kunkel, Joseph A., III. 1988. "Party Endorsement and Incumbency in Minnesota Legislative Nominations." *Legislative Studies Quarterly* 13(2):211–223.

Kunovich, Sheri, and Pamela Paxton. 2005. "Pathways to Power: The Role of Political Parties in Women's National Political Representation." *American Journal of Sociology* 111(2):505–552.

Kurtz, Karl T., Bruce E. Cain, and Richard G. Niemi, eds. 2007. *Institutional Change in American Politics: The Case of Term Limits*. Ann Arbor: University of Michigan Press.

Larimer, Christopher W., Rebecca J. Hannagan, and Kevin B. Smith. 2007. "Balancing Ambition and Gender among Decision Makers." *Annals of the American Academy of Political and Social Science* 614(56–73).

Larsson, Einar. 1996. "Einar Larsson." In Lars Gustafsson, ed., *Riksdagsutskotten inifrån: Tretton ledamöters hågkomster*. Stockholm: Riksbankens Jubileumsfond/Gidlunds Förlag.

Lasswell, Harold D. 1930. *Psychopathology and Politics*. Chicago: University of Chicago Press.

Lawless, Jennifer L., and Richard L. Fox. 2005. *It Takes a Candidate: Why Women Still Don't Run for Office*. New York: Cambridge University Press.

———. 2010. *It Still Takes a Candidate: Why Women Still Don't Run for Office*. New York: Cambridge University Press.

Lawless, Jennifer L., and Kathryn Pearson. 2008. "The Primary Reason for Women's Under-Representation: Re-Evaluating the Conventional Wisdom." *Journal of Politics* 70(1):67–82.

Lawless, Jennifer L., and Sean M. Theriault. 2005. "Women in the US Congress: From Entry to Exit." In Lois Duke Whitaker, ed., *Women in Politics: Outsiders or Insiders?* New York: Prentice Hall.

Leib, Prudence. 1990. "The Origins of Ambition." In Arnold I. Goldberg, ed., *The Realities of Transference: Progress in Self Psychology*, Vol. 6. Hillsdale, NJ: Analytic Press.

Leijon, Anna-Greta. 1991. *Alla rosor ska inte tuktas*. Stockholm: Tidens Förlag.

Leuthold, David A. 1968. *Electioneering in a Democracy*. New York: Wiley.

Levine, Martin D., and Mark S. Hyde. 1977. "Incumbency and the Theory of Political Ambition: Rational Choice Model." *Journal of Politics* 39:959–983.

Liebig, Brigitte. 2000. "Perspectives on Gender Cultures in Elites." In Mino Vianello and Gwen Moore, eds., *Gendering Elites: Economic and Political Leadership in 27 Industrialized Societies.* London: MacMillan.

Lijphart, Arend. 1984. *Democracies: Patterns of Majoritarian and Consensus Government in Twenty-one Countries.* New Haven, CT: Yale University Press.

———. 1990. "The Political Consequences of Electoral Laws, 1945–1985." *American Political Science Review* 84(2):481–496.

———. 1999. *Patterns of Democracy: Government Forms and Performance in Thirty-six Countries.* New Haven, CT: Yale University Press.

Lindstädt, René, and Ryan J. Vander Wielen. 2014. "Dynamic Elite Partisanship: Party Loyalty and Agenda Setting in the US House." *British Journal of Political Science* 44(4):741–772.

Lindström, Ulla. 1970. *Och regeringen satt kvar!: Ur min politiska dagbok 1960–1967.* Stockholm: Bonniers.

Lovenduski, Joni, and Pippa Norris, eds. 1993. *Gender and Party Politics.* London: Sage.

Lublin, David I. 1994. "Quality, Not Quantity: Strategic Politicians in US Senate Elections, 1952–1990." *Journal of Politics* 56(1):228–241.

Luskin, Robert C. 1990. "Explaining Political Sophistication." *Political Behavior* 12(4):331–361.

Macdonald, Stuart Elaine. 1987. *Political Ambition and Attainment: A Dynamic Analysis of Parliamentary Careers.* Ann Arbor: University of Michigan.

Machiavelli, Niccolò. 2001. *The Prince.* Translated by N. H. Thomson. The Harvard Classics, Vol. 36, Part 1. Bartleby.com. First published 1909 by P. F. Collier and Son. 1909.

Madestam, Jenny. 2009. *En kompispappa och en ytlig djuping: Partieliters ambivalenta partiledarideal.* Stockholm: Stockholm University.

Madison, James. 1788. "The Structure of the Government Must Furnish the Proper Checks and Balances between the Different Departments." *The Federalist Papers No. 51.* https://www.congress.gov/resources/display/content/The+Federalist+Papers#TheFederalist Papers-51.

Maestas, Cherie D. 2000. "Professional Legislatures and Ambitious Politicians: Policy Responsiveness of State Institutions." *Legislative Studies Quarterly* 25(4):663–690.

———. 2003. "The Incentive to Listen: Progressive Ambition, Resources, and Opinion Monitoring among State Legislators." *Journal of Politics* 65(2):439–456.

Maestas, Cherie D., et al. 2006. "When to Risk It? Institutions, Ambitions, and the Decision to Run for the US House." *American Political Science Review* 100(2):195–208.

Mair, Peter. 1994. "Party Organizations: From Civil Society to the State." In Richard S. Katz and Peter Mair, eds., *Party Organization in Western Democracies.* London: Sage.

Maisel, L. Sandy, and Walter J. Stone. 1997. "Determinants of Candidate Emergence in US House Elections: An Exploratory Study." *Legislative Studies Quarterly* 22(1):79–96.

Manin, Bernard. 1996. *The Principles of Representative Government.* Cambridge: Cambridge University Press.

Martin, Shane. 2008. "Two Houses: Legislative Studies and the Atlantic Divide." *PS: Political Science & Politics* 41(3):557–565. Estimates against Policy Series. *Electoral Studies* 26(1):121–129.

———. 2011. "Using Parliamentary Questions to Measure Constituency Focus: An Application to the Irish Case." *Political Studies* 59(2):472–488.

Matland, Richard E., and Donley T. Studlar. 2004. "Determinants of Legislative Turnover: A Cross-National Analysis." *British Journal of Political Science* 34(1):87–108.

Matthews, Donald R. 1954. *The Social Background of Political Decision-Makers.* New York: Random House.

———. 1959. "The Folkways of the United States Senate: Conformity to Group Norms and Legislative Effectiveness." *American Political Science Review* 53(4):1064–1089.

———. 1960. *US Senators and Their World.* New York: Vintage.

Mayhew, David R. 1974. *Congress: The Electoral Connection.* New Haven, CT: Yale University Press.

McAdams, John C., and John R. Johannes. 1987. "Determinants of Spending by House Challengers, 1974–84." *American Journal of Political Science* 31(3):457–483.

McAllister, Ian, and Donley T. Studlar. 2002. "Electoral Systems and Women's Representation: A Long-Term Perspective." *Representation* 39(1):3–14.

McCain, John, and Mark Salter. 2002. *Worth the Fighting For: A Memoir.* New York: Random House.

McCrae, Robert R., and Paul T. Costa Jr. 1999. "A Five-Factor Theory of Personality." In Lawrence A. Pervin and Oliver P. John, eds., *Handbook of Personality: Theory and Research,* 2nd ed. New York: Guilford.

McLoyd, Vonnie C. 1998. "Socioeconomic Disadvantage and Child Development." *American Psychologist* 53(2):185–204.

Meserve, Stephen A., Daniel Pemstein, and William T. Bernhard. 2009. "Political Ambition and Legislative Behavior in the European Parliament." *The Journal of Politics* 71(3): 1015–1032.

Messick, David M., and Charles G. McClintock. 1968. "Motivational Bases of Choice in Experimental Games." *Journal of Experimental Social Psychology* 4(1):1–25.

Mezey, Michael L. 1970. "Ambition Theory and the Office of Congressmen." *Journal of Politics* 32(3):563.

Milinski, Manfred, Dirk Semmann, and Hans-Jürgen Krambeck. 2002. "Reputation Helps Solve the 'Tragedy of the Commons.'" *Nature* 415:424–426.

Moncrief, Gary F., Peverill Squire, and Malcolm E. Jewell. 2001. *Who Runs for the Legislature?* Upper Saddle River, NJ: Prentice Hall.

Mondak, Jeffery J. 2010. *Personality and the Foundations of Political Behavior.* New York: Cambridge University Press.

Moore, Michael K., and John R. Hibbing. 1992. "Is Serving in Congress Fun Again? Voluntary Retirement from the House since the 1970s." *American Journal of Political Science* 36(3):824–828.

———. 1998. "Situational Dissatisfaction in Congress: Explaining Voluntary Departures." *Journal of Politics* 60(4):1088–1107.

Newton, Kenneth. 2007. "Social and Political Trust." In Russel J. Dalton and Hans-Dieter Klingemann, eds. *The Oxford Handbook of Political Behaviour.* Oxford: Oxford University Press.

Ng, Thomas W. H., et al. 2005. "Predictors of Objective and Subjective Career Success: A Meta-Analysis." *Personnel Psychology* 58:367–408.

Nielsen, Peder. 2001. "På och av—om uppdragsvillighet, rekrytering och avhopp i den kommunala demokratin." Swedish Government Report SOU 2001:48. Stockholm: Fritzes.

Niklasson, Birgitta. 2005. *Contact Capital in Political Careers: Gender and Recruitment of Parliamentarians and Political Appointees.* Gothenburg: University of Gothenburg.

Norris, Pippa. 1985. "Women's Legislative Participation in Western Europe." *West European Politics* 8:90–101.

———. 1996. "Legislative Recruitment." In Lawrence LeDuc, Richard G. Niemi, and Pippa Norris, eds., *Comparing Democracies: Elections and Voting in Global Perspective.* London: Sage.

———, ed. 1997. *Passage to Power: Legislative Recruitment in Advanced Democracies.* Cambridge: Cambridge University Press.

Norris, Pippa, and Joni Lovenduski. 1995. *Political Recruitment: Gender, Race, and Class in the British Parliament.* Cambridge: Cambridge University Press.

Öhberg, Patrik, and Lena Wängnerud. 2014. "Testing the Impact of Political Generations: The Class of '94 and Pro Feminist Ideas in the Swedish Riksdag." *Scandinavian Political Studies* 37(1):61–81.

Okimoto, Tyler G., and Victoria L. Brescoll. 2010. "The Price of Power: Power Seeking and Backlash against Female Politicians." *Personality and Social Psychology Bulletin* 36(7):923–936.

Ordeshook, Peter C., and Olga V. Shvetsova. 1994. "Ethnic Heterogeneity, District Magnitude, and the Number of Parties." *American Journal of Political Science* 38(1):100–123.

Oscarsson, Henrik, and Sören Holmberg. 2013. *Nya svenska väljare.* Stockholm: Nordstedts Juridik.

Oskarson, Maria, and Lena Wängnerud. 1995. *Kvinnor som väljare och valda.* Lund: Studentlitteratur.

Ozer, Daniel J., and Veronica Benet-Martinez. 2006. "Personality and the Prediction of Consequential Outcomes." *Annual Review of Psychology* 57:401–421.

Panebianco, Angelo. 1988. *Political Parties: Organization and Power.* Cambridge: Cambridge University Press.

Pareto, Vilfredo. 1935. *The Mind and Society.* London: Jonathan Cape.

Parker, Glenn R., and Suzanne L. Parker. 1985. "Correlates and Effects of Attention to District by US House Members." *Legislative Studies Quarterly* 10(2):223–242.

Patzelt, Werner J. 1999. "Recruitment and Retention in Western European Parliaments." *Legislative Studies Quarterly* 24(2):239–279.

Payne, James L., and Oliver H. Woshinsky. 1972. "Incentives for Political Participation." *World Politics* 24(4):518–546.

Payne, James L., et al. 1984. *The Motivation of Politicians.* Chicago: Nelson-Hall.

Paxton, Pamela. 1997. "Women in National Legislatures: A Cross-National Analysis." *Social Science Research* 26(4):442–464.

Paxton, Pamela, Melanie M. Hughes, and Matthew A. Painter. 2010. "Growth in Women's

Political Representation: A Longitudinal Exploration of Democracy, Electoral System and Gender Quotas." *European Journal of Political Research* 49(1):25–52.

Persson, Torsten, and Guido Tabellini. 1994. "Is Inequality Harmful for Growth?" *American Economic Review* 84(3):600–621.

Persson, Torsten, Guido Tabellini, and Francesco Trebbi. 2003. "Electoral Rules and Corruption." *Journal of the European Economic Association* 1(4):958–989.

Petersson, Olof, et al. 1997. *Demokratirådets rapport 1997: Demokrati och ledarskap.* Stockholm: SNS Förlag.

Petersson, Olof, ed. 1998. *Demokratirådets rapport 1998: Demokrati och medborgarskap.* Kristianstad: SNS Förlag.

Pettigrove, Glen. 2007. "Ambitions." *Ethical Theory and Moral Practice* 10(1):53–68.

Pierre, Jon, ed. 2016. *The Oxford Handbook of Swedish Politics.* Oxford: Oxford University Press.

Pitkin, Hanna Fenichel. 1967. *The Concept of Representation.* Berkeley: University of California Press.

Plato. 1987. *The Republic.* London: Penguin Classics.

Pollak, Johannes. 2007. "Contested Meanings of Representation." *Comparative European Politics* 5(1):87–103.

Pomper, Gerald M. 1975. "Ambition in Israel: A Comparative Extension of Theory and Data." *Western Political Quarterly* 28(4):712–732.

Prewitt, Kenneth. 1970. *The Recruitment of Political Leaders: A Study of Citizen-Politicians.* Indianapolis, IN: Bobbs-Merrill.

Prewitt, Kenneth, Heinz Eulau, and Betty H. Zisk. 1966. "Political Socialization and Political Roles." *Public Opinion Quarterly* 30(4):569–582.

Przeworski, Adam, Susan C. Stokes, and Bernard Manin, eds. 1999. *Democracy, Accountability, and Representation.* Cambridge: Cambridge University Press.

Putnam, Robert D. 1976. *The Comparative Study of Political Elites.* Englewood Cliffs, NJ: Prentice-Hall.

———. 1993. *Making Democracy Work: Civic Traditions in Modern Italy.* Princeton, NJ: Princeton University Press.

Rehfeld, Andrew. 2009. "Representation Rethought: On Trustees, Delegates, and Gyroscopes in the Study of Political Representation and Democracy." *American Political Science Review* 103(2):214–230.

Reichley, James. 2000. *The Life of the Parties: A History of American Political Parties.* Lanham, MD: Rowman and Littlefield.

Reynolds, Andrew. 1999. "Women in the Legislatures and Executives of the World." *World Politics* 51(4):547–572.

Riker, William H. 1962. *A Theory of Political Coalitions.* New Haven, CT: Yale University Press.

Roback, Thomas H. 1975. "Amateurs and Professionals: Delegates to the 1972 Republican National Convention." *Journal of Politics* 37(2):436–468.

Robeck, Bruce W. 1982. "State Legislator Candidacies for the US House: Prospects for Success." *Legislative Studies Quarterly* 7(4):507–514.

Rohde, David W. 1979. "Risk-Bearing and Progressive Ambition: The Case of Members of the United States House of Representatives." *American Journal of Political Science* 23:1–26.

Rothstein, Bo, and Eric M. Uslaner. 2005. "All for All: Equality, Corruption, and Social Trust." *World Politics* 58(1):41–72.

Rule, Wilma. 1987. "Electoral Systems, Contextual Factors, and Women's Opportunity for Election to Parliament in Twenty-three Democracies." *Western Political Quarterly* 40(3):477–498.

Sartori, Giovanni. 1976. *Parties and Party Systems*. New York: Cambridge University Press.

Scarrow, Susan E. 1997. "Political Career Paths and the European Parliament." *Legislative Studies Quarterly* 22(2):253–263.

Schäfer, Armin. 2010. "Consequences of Social Inequality for Democracy in Western Europe." *Zeitschrift für Vergleichende Politikwissenschaft*.

Schlaug, Birger. 2002. "Mitt farväl till politiken." *Borås Tidning*, 18 January.

Schlesinger, Joseph A. 1966. *Ambition and Politics: Political Careers in the United States*. Chicago: Rand McNally.

———. 1985. "The New American Political Party." *American Political Science Review* 79(4):1152–1169.

———. 1994. *Political Parties and the Winning of Office*. Ann Arbor: University of Michigan Press.

Schmitt, Hermann, and Jacobus Johannes Adrianus Thomassen, eds. 1999. *Political Representation and Legitimacy in the European Union*. Oxford: Oxford University Press.

Schoon, Ingrid, Andy Ross, and Peter Martin. 2007. "Science Related Careers, Aspirations and Outcomes in Two British Cohort Studies." *Equal Opportunities International* 26(2):129–148.

Schumpeter, Joseph A. 1942. *Capitalism, Socialism and Democracy*. New York: Harper and Row.

Schunk, Dale H., and Marsha W. Lilly. 1984. "Sex Differences in Self-Efficacy and Attributions: Influence of Performance Feedback." *Journal of Early Adolescence* 4(3):203–213.

Searing, Donald D. 1991. "Roles, Rules, and Rationality in the New Institutionalism." *American Political Science Review* 85(4):1239–1260.

———. 1994. *Westminster's World: Understanding Political Roles*. Cambridge, MA: Harvard University Press.

Seligman, Adam B. 1997. *The Problem of Trust*. Princeton, NJ: Princeton University Press.

Shepsle, Kenneth A. 1985. "Prospects for Formal Models of Legislatures." *Legislative Studies Quarterly* 10(1):5–19.

Shields, Todd G., and Robert K. Goidel. 1997. "Participation Rates, Socioeconomic Class Biases, and Congressional Elections: A Cross Validation." *American Journal of Political Science* 41(3):683–691.

Sieberer, Ulrich, and Wolfgang C. Müller. 2015. "Aiming Higher: The Consequences of Progressive Ambition among MPs in European Parliaments." *European Political Science Review* 1:1–24.

Siegfried, André. 1913. *Tableau politique de la France de l'Ouest sous la Troisieme Republique*. Paris: Colin.

Sirin, Selcuk R. 2005. "Socioeconomic Status and Academic Achievement: A Meta-Analytic Review of Research." *Review of Educational Research* 75(3):417–453.

Sjöblom, Gunnar. 1968. *Party Strategies in a Multiparty System.* Lund: Lund University Press.

Smith, Kevin B., et al. 2007. "Evolutionary Theory and Political Leadership: Why Certain People Do Not Trust Decision Makers." *Journal of Politics* 69(2):285–299.

Sorauf, Frank Joseph. 1963. *Party and Representation.* New York: Atherton.

Sorokin, Pitirim Aleksandrovich. 1927. *Social Mobility.* New York: Harper.

Soule, John W. 1969. "Future Political Ambitions and the Behavior of Incumbent State Legislators." *Midwest Journal of Political Science* 13(3):439–454.

Southwell, Priscilla L. 1986. "The Politics of Disgruntlement: Nonvoting and Defection among Supporters of Nomination Losers, 1968–1984." *Political Behavior* 8:81–95.

Squire, Peverill. 1989. "Competition and Uncontested Seats in US House Elections." *Legislative Studies Quarterly* 14(2):281–295.

Stone, Walter J., and L. Sandy Maisel. 2003. "The Not-So-Simple Calculus of Winning: Potential US House Candidates' Nominations and General Election Prospects." *Journal of Politics* 65(4):951–977.

Stouten, Jeroen, David De Cremer, and Eric Van Dijk. 2005. "All Is Well That Ends Well, at Least for Proselfs: Emotional Reactions to Equality Violation as a Function of Social Value Orientation." *European Journal of Social Psychology* 35(6):767–783.

Strand, Dieter. 1980. *Palme igen?: scener ur en partiledares liv.* Stockholm: Norstedt.

Strøm, Kaare. 1990. "A Behavioral Theory of Competitive Political Parties." *American Journal of Political Science* 34(2):565–598.

———. 1997. "Rules, Reasons, and Routines: Legislative Roles in Parliamentary Democracies." In Wolfgang C. Müller and Thomas Saalfeld, eds., *Members of Parliament in Western Europe: Roles and Behavior.* London: Cass.

Sullivan, Vickie B. 2006. *Machiavelli, Hobbes, and the Formation of a Liberal Republicanism in England.* Cambridge: Cambridge University Press.

Svensson, Alf. 2001. *Här kommer Alf Svensson: Minnen.* Stockholm: Bonnier.

Swedish Government Report SOU 1990:44. *Demokrati och makt i Sverige.* Principal Report of the Public Inquiry on Power.

Swedish Government Report SOU 2007:108. *Gender, makt och statistik.* Stockholm: Fritzes Förlag.

Taagepera, Rein, and Matthew Soberg Shugart. 1989. *Seats and Votes: The Effects and Determinants of Electoral Systems.* New Haven, CT: Yale University Press.

Ternström, Solveig. 2009. "Politik viktigare än karriär för oss äldre." *Expressen,* 10 June.

Tingsten, Herbert. 1937. *Political Behavior: Studies in Election Statistics.* London: P. S. King.

Treul, Sarah A. 2009. "Ambition and Party Loyalty in the US Senate." *American Politics Research* 37(3):449–464.

Tricomi, Elizabeth, et al. 2010. "Neural Evidence for Inequality-Averse Social Preferences." *Nature* 463(7284):1089–1091.

Troy, Gil. 1996. *See How They Ran: The Changing Role of the Presidential Candidate.* Cambridge, MA: Harvard University Press.

Turner, Charles F., Judith T. Lessler, and James Devore. 1992. "Effects of Mode of Administration and Wording on Reporting of Drug Use." In Charles F. Turner, Judith T. Lessler, and Joseph C. Gfroerer, eds., *Survey Measurement of Drug Use: Methodological Studies.* DHHS Publication (ADM)92-1929. Rockville, MD: National Institution on Drug Abuse.

Turner, Charles F., Heather G. Miller, and Lincoln E. Moses, eds. 1990. "Methodological Issues in AIDS Surveys." In *AIDS: The Second Decade.* Washington, DC: National Academy Press.

Van Der Slik, Jack R., and Samuel J. Pernacciaro. 1979. "Office Ambitions and Voting Behavior in the US Senate." *American Politics Quarterly* 7:198–224.

Van Dijk, Eric, and David De Cremer. 2006. "Self-Benefiting in the Allocation of Scarce Resources: Leader-Follower Effects and the Moderating Effect of Social Value Orientations." *Personality and Social Psychology Bulletin* 32(10):1352–1361.

Van Hiel, Alain, Malgorzata Kossowska, and Ivan Mervielde. 2000. "The Relationship between Openness to Experience and Political Ideology." *Personality and Individual Differences* 28(4):741–751.

Van Vugt, Mark. 2006. "Evolutionary Origins of Leadership and Followership." *Personality and Social Psychology Review* 10(4):354–371.

Verba, Sidney, Kay L. Schlozman, and Henry E. Brady. 1995. *Voice and Equality: Civic Voluntarism in American Politics.* Cambridge, MA: Harvard University Press.

Wahlke, John C., et al. 1962. *The Legislative System: Explorations in Legislative Behavior.* New York: John Wiley.

Wängnerud, Lena. 1998. *Politikens andra sida: om kvinnorepresentation i Sveriges riksdag.* Gothenburg: Department of Political Science, University of Gothenburg.

———. 2009. "Women in Parliaments: Descriptive and Substantive Representation." *Annual Review of Political Science* 12:51–69.

———. 2015. *The Principles of Gender-Sensitive Parliaments.* London: Routledge.

Warren, Mark, and Jane Mansbridge. 2013. "Deliberative Negotiation." In Jane Mansbridge and Cathie Jo Martin, eds., *Negotiating Agreement in Politics: Report of the Task Force on Negotiating Agreement in Politics.* Washington, DC: American Political Science Association.

Welzel, Christian. 2009. "Political Culture." In Todd Landman and Neil Robinson, eds., *The Sage Handbook of Comparative Politics.* London: Sage.

Weststeijn, Arthur. 2010. "From the Passion of Self-Love to the Virtue of Self-Interest: The Republican Morals of the Brothers De la Court." *European Review of History* 17(1):75–92.

Whistler, Donald E., and Mark C. Ellickson. 2010. "A Rational Choice Approach to Explaining Policy Preferences and Concern for Representing Women among State Legislators." *Politics & Policy* 38(1):25–51.

White, Alastair T. 1982. "Why Community Participation? A Discussion of the Arguments." *Assignment Children* 59/60:17–34.

White, Thomas I. 1982. "Pride and the Public Good: Thomas More's Use of Plato in Utopia." *Journal of the History of Philosophy* 20(4):329–354.

Wibble, Anne. 1994. *Två cigg och en kopp kaffe.* Stockholm: Ekerlids Förlag.

Wolfinger, Raymond E., and Steven J. Rosenstone. 1980. *Who Votes?* New Haven, CT: Yale University Press.

Woodward, Bob. 1996. *The Choice: How Clinton Won*. New York. Simon and Schuster.
Wrighton, J. Mark, and Peverill Squire. 1997. "Uncontested Seats and Electoral Competition for the US House of Representatives Over Time." *Journal of Politics* 59(2):452–468.

OTHER SOURCES

Dagens Nyheter (15 September 2008): "Partipiskan biter sämre på folkvald"
Fokus (29 May 2009): "Politiker flyr till Bryssel"
Statistics Sweden database
Svenska Dagbladet (11 March 2011): "Frågan höll mig vaken"
Swedish Election Authority website
Swedish Riksdag website

INDEX

socioeconomic resources, *continued*
  attitudes toward high-status positions
    and, 79(table), 80
  career ambitions and, 40–45, 46(table),
    52–55, 53(table), 85, 115
  education levels, 41–42, 43, 73, 109–110
  political participation and, 38, 39
Soule, John W., 64
Spain, ambitious politicians, 102, 103(table),
    104(table)
status of political positions
  career success measures, 95–97,
    96(table)
  moving to higher-status institutions, 24,
    28–29
  ranking, 79–80, 88, 90–91
Stockholm area, ambitious politicians in,
    49–50, 50(table), 54
Stolz, Klaus, 17
Sträng, Gunnar, 9, 10
Strøm, Kaare, 63
Support Stockings movement, 86–87
Svensson, Alf, 9
Sweden
  cabinet ministers, 9, 29, 80, 91, 128n1,
    129n4
  cities, 49–50
  gender quotas, 76–77, 77(table), 81
  local politicians, 41, 47, 48, 87, 116
  military signals intelligence, 70–71
  parties, 8, 9–10
  party-centered political culture, 1–2, 8–10,
    27
  political ambition research, 16–17
  political culture, 107, 118
  political system, 8–9, 125n7
  prime ministers, 9, 10, 87, 90, 132n5
  unambitious politicians, 8, 9–10, 26–27,
    117, 128n11
Swedish Election Authority, 92, 93
Swedish MPs
  age differences, 58
  ages at entry to parliament, 85, 86(table),
    87
  campaigns, 67
  committee seats, 84, 87–89, 88(table),
    89(table)

education levels, 41, 73, 109–110
gender differences, 41
interest in constituencies, 56, 61–62, 63,
    64–67, 81, 130nn8–9
interest in international issues, 65–67,
    66(table), 82
job satisfaction, 128n3
language skills, 45, 54
occupations, 44, 110
professionalization, 115–116
reasons for leaving office, 50, 92–95,
    94(table)
regions of residence, 49–50, 54
religiosity, 44
salaries, 115
socioeconomic status, 42, 110
support for European Union, 103
swiftness to parliament, 85–87, 86(table)
votes, 70–72, 71(table)
women, 41, 85–87, 97–98, 127n7
See also Parliamentary Studies
Swedish MPs, career ambitions of
  attitudes toward high-status positions
    and, 77–80, 78(table), 79(table), 88
  attitudes toward party norms and, 59,
    68(table), 68–69, 69(table)
  attitudes toward representation and, 59,
    61–67, 62(table), 65(table), 81, 82, 113
  behaviors, 55, 56–58, 59–61, 63, 67–68,
    69–76, 80–81, 119
  career attainment and, 84–91, 95–100,
    96(table), 98(table), 101, 113–114
  commitment to, 30, 34–35
  common attributes and, 37
  differences from unambitious MPs, 81–82,
    121
  early engagement and, 46–48
  empirical indicator, 26, 30–32, 31(table),
    32(table), 35–36
  European context, 101–105, 110–111, 114
  first-term members, 30, 34–35, 35(table),
    119, 128–129n5
  in future, 116–117
  goals beyond parliament, 81–82, 119–120
  inside games, 72–76, 73(table), 113
  inside parliament, 31–32, 32(table), 35,
    35(table), 119

issue positions and, 76–77, 77(table)
lack of, 26–27
negative views of, 27, 60
outside games, 73–74
by party membership, 50–52, 51(table)
potential, 37, 42–55
real, 56, 80–82
recruitment and, 48–49, 49(table), 54
reluctance to discuss, 9–10, 22, 27, 90
retention of seats and, 60, 84–85, 90,
    91–95, 92(table), 95(table), 116
socioeconomic resources and, 40–45,
    46(table), 52–55, 53(table), 85, 115
survey questions, 26, 27–31, 32–34
temporal aspect, 33–34, 34(table)
theoretical definition, 27–30

term limits, 106
Ternström, Solveig, 58
Thomas Aquinas, 6, 23
Tocqueville, Alexis de, 23

unambitious politicians
    differences from ambitious, 81–82, 121
    in Norway, 22
    in Sweden, 8, 9–10, 26–27, 117, 128n11
    in the United States, 7–8
United States
    ambitious politicians, 1, 7–8, 10–11, 82, 112,
        122
    gender differences in ambition, 41
    political career paths, 17–18
    political culture, 3–4, 114
    Republican Party, 19, 131n16

state legislators, 49, 64, 106
term limits, 106
unambitious politicians, 7–8
US Congress
    ambitious members, 1, 2–4, 21, 99, 114–115
    behaviors of members, 21, 56–57
    first-term members, 130n3
    interest in constituencies, 61–63, 67
    party leadership and, 4
    Republican Party control, 131n16
    reputations of senators, 58–59

Vander Wielen, Ryan J., 4
Verba, Sidney, 39, 43–45, 52
voluntarism. See Civic Voluntarism Model
    (CVM)
voluntary organizations, 44
voters, politicians' interactions with, 63, 66,
    67

Wängnerud, Lena, 11
Wibble, Anne, 9
Wijkman, Anders, 10
Wilson, Woodrow, 14–15
women
    cabinet ministers, 9, 29, 128n1, 129n4
    candidates, 131n17
    local politicians, 87
    Members of Parliament, 107, 109, 129n3
    networks, 41
    political cultures and, 106–107
    Swedish MPs, 41, 85–87, 97–98, 127n7
    in US legislatures, 19–20
    See also gender differences